THE PILGRIM'S
GUIDE TO ROME

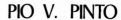

PIO V. PINTO

THE PILGRIM'S GUIDE TO ROME

HARPER & ROW, PUBLISHERS
NEW YORK, EVANSTON,
SAN FRANCISCO, LONDON

© Nardini Editore — Centro Internazionale del Libro S.p.A. Firenze (Italia) 1974.

FIRST U.S. EDITION 1975

ISBN: 0-06-013388-0

LIBRARY OF CONGRESS CATALOG CARD NUMBER: 74-24852

Made and printed in Italy

First published in the English language in Italy under the title « Quo Vadis? ».

ROME, CITY OF FAITH

The Holy Year, proclaimed by Pope Paul VI, in its local celebration in 1974 in the individual Dioceses has certainly brought the people of God, reunited around their Bishop, to a better comprehension of its great spiritual values: renewal of life and reconciliation with God and with their fellow-man.

However, the pilgrimage to Rome in 1975 always remains the most significant expression of the goal of the path of Faith: the meeting with God the Father, together with brothers of all of the world in charity, in reconciliation, and in peace, crowned by the gift of Holy Year Indulgence.

Rome, in fact, is above all the City of the Spirit for pilgrims—a center of unity, a fresh and living source of Faith. In Rome will take place the meeting with « Peter », the Pope, to whom is entrusted the task « to confirm the brothers in the Faith ».

In our modern, technical and consumer society, to still be able to discover the memories of the Apostles Peter and Paul, the faith of the Martyrs and the examples of the Saints which characterize the history of Rome, will be the same as finding again the ways of Hope and Charity, the ways of peace.

Rome, May 23, 1974
Ascension Day

Cardinal Ugo Poletti
Vicar General for His Holiness for Rome

BULL OF INDICTION
OF
THE HOLY YEAR 1975

PAUL

SERVANT OF THE SERVANTS
OF GOD TO ALL THE FAITHFUL:
HEALTH AND THE
APOSTOLIC BLESSING

THE MEMORIALS OF THE APOSTLES, the holy places of Rome where there are worthily preserved and religiously venerated the tombs of the Apostles Peter and Paul, those « holy fathers » through whom the City became not only the « disciple of truth » but also the teacher of truth and the centre of Catholic unity, now—as the universal Jubilee to be celebrated there approaches—shine forth more brightly to the minds of the faithful as the goal of pilgrimage.

Down the centuries, these memorials have always impelled the Christian people to be fervent in their faith and to testify to ecclesial communion. This is so because the Church recognizes her identity and the cause of her unity in the foundation laid by Jesus Christ, namely, the Apostles. From as early as the second century the faithful came to Rome to see and venerate the « trophies » of the Apostles Peter and Paul in those very places where they are preserved; and they made pilgrimages to the Church of Rome to contemplate her « regal dignity ». In the fourth century the pilgrimage to Rome became the principal form in the West of that kind of religious journey. It was similar to, and had the same religious purpose as, the pilgrimage which was made in the East to Jerusalem where the Lord's sepulchre is found. In the early Middle Ages there came on pilgrimage to Rome from various parts of Europe, and even from the East, those who were « linked to the Chair of Peter », especially monks, and who wished to make a profession of their orthodox faith at the tombs of the Apostles.

The idea of a pilgrimage increased further from the twelfth to the thirteenth century, becoming all the more common by reason of a renewal of spirituality and popular piety which spread throughout Europe at that time. This renewal served to enrich the ancient notion which the Church received from tradition and which was equally to be found in other religions, namely, the concept of a « pilgrimage undertaken for the love of God ». In this way the Jubilee Year originated: it was as if it were the result of a process of maturing in the doctrinal, biblical and theological fields. It emerged plainly for the first time in the year 1220, when our predecessor Honorius III proclaimed a Jubilee Year for the pilgrimage to the tomb of Saint Thomas Becket. Later, as is well known, pilgrims came to Rome to the Basilicas of Saint Peter and Saint Paul, in the great popular and penitential movement of the year 1300, a movement confirmed by our predecessor Boniface VIII, and which was marked by a longing to obtain pardon from God and peace among men. This movement was directed to this very lofty motive: « the glory of God and the exaltation of the faith ».

The Roman Jubilee of 1300 was the beginning and the pattern of those which have followed (every twenty-five years from the fifteenth century onwards, except when the series was interrupted by extraneous circumstances). This is an indication of the continuity and vitality which have always confirmed the relevance of this venerable institution for every age.

It is correct to say that the Jubilees celebrated in recent times have preserved this outstanding value, whereby the unity and renewal of the Church are affirmed in a special way and all men encouraged to recognize one another as brothers and to walk in the path of peace. Such a desire manifested itself at the beginning of this century, when our predecessor Leo XIII proclaimed the Jubilee Year in 1900. The human family was filled with the same hopes and expectations when, a quarter of a century later, afflicted by grave dangers and contention, it awaited the special Holy Year of 1933 on the occasion of the nineteenth centenary of the Redemption. It was the same noble aspirations for justice and peaceful coexistence among men that Pius XII put forward in the last Jubilee, in the year 1950.

It seems to us that in the present Holy Year all the principal and important motives of the previous Jubilees are present and expressed in summary form in the themes that we ourself laid down in our discourse of 9 May 1973 when we first announced the Holy Year: renewal and reconciliation. We have offered these themes for the reflection of the pastors and faithful, particularly during the anticipated celebration of the Jubilee in the local Churches, and we have added to them our exhortations and our catechesis. But the aspirations that the two themes enunciate and the lofty ideals that they express will find a more complete realization in Rome, where the pilgrims to the Tombs of the Apostles Peter and Paul and to the memorials of the other martyrs will come more easily into contact with the ancient sources of the Church's faith and life, in order to be converted by repentance, strengthened in charity and united more closely with their brethren by the grace of God.

This renewal and reconciliation pertain in the first place to the interior life, above all because it is in the depths of the heart that there exists the root of all good and, unfortunately, of all evil. It is in the depths of the heart therefore that there must take place conversion or *metanoia*, that is, a change of direction, of attitude, of option, of one's way of life.

. . . .

For this reason, interpreting as it were the Church's maternal sentiments, we impart the gift of the Plenary Indulgence to all the faithful who are properly disposed, and who, after confessing their sins and receiving Holy Communion, pray for

the intentions of the Supreme Pontiff and the College of Bishops:
1) if they undertake a sacred pilgrimage to one of the Patriarchal Basilicas (the Basilica of Saint Peter's in the Vatican, Saint Paul's Outside-the-Walls, the Lateran Archbasilica of the Most Holy Saviour, or Saint Mary Major's), or to some other church or place of the City of Rome designated by the competent authority, and there devoutly take part in a liturgical celebration, especially the Sacrifice of the Mass, or some exercise of piety (e. g. the Way of the Cross, the Rosary);
2) if they visit, in a group or individually, one of the four Patriarchal Basilicas and there spend some time in devout recollection concluding with the Our Father, the Profession of Faith in any approved form and a prayer to the Blessed Virgin Mary;
3) if, being prevented by illness or some other grave reason from going on a pilgrimage to Rome, they unite themselves spiritually with this pilgrimage and offer their prayers and sufferings to God;
4) if, being prevented while in Rome by illness or some other grave reason from taking part in a liturgical celebration or exercise of piety or visit made by their group (ecclesial, family or social, as mentioned in 1) and 2) above), they unite themselves spiritually with the group and offer their prayers and sufferings to God.

During the Holy Year moreover there remain in force the other concessions of indulgences, with the proviso as before that a plenary indulgence can be gained only once a day; however, all indulgences can always be applied to the dead in *mundum suffragii*.

. . . .

As is well known, in recent years one of the Church's most pressing concerns has been to disseminate everywhere a message of charity, of social awareness and of peace, and to promote, as far as she can, works of justice and of solidarity in favour of all those in need, of those on the

7

margins of society, of exiles and of the oppressed — in favour of all men, in fact, whether individuals, social groups or peoples. We earnestly desire therefore that the Holy Year, through the works of charity which it suggests to the faithful and which it asks of them, should be an opportune time for strengthening and supporting the moral consciousness of all the faithful and of that wider community of all men which the message of the Church can reach if an earnest effort is made

We wish, however, to invite all the sons and daughters of the Church, and especially the pilgrims coming to Rome, to undertake certain definite tasks which, as successor of Peter and head of that Church « which presides over the universal gathering of charity » we now publicly propose and commend to all. We refer to the carrying out of works of faith and charity for the benefit of our needy brethren in Rome and in other Churches of the world. These works will not necessarily be grandiose ones, although such are in no way to be excluded. In many cases what are today called « micro-realizations » will be sufficient, corresponding as they do to the Gospel spirit of charity. In this field the Church, in view of the modest resources at her disposal, will perhaps have to limit herself more and more to giving men nothing more than the widow's mite. But she knows and teaches that the good which counts most is that which, in humble and very often unknown ways, manages to give help where there is a little need and to heal small wounds — things which often find no place in large projects of social reform.

Finally, we wish to proclaim and preach that the reconciliation of Christians is one of the principal aims of the Holy Year. However, before all men can be brought together and restored to the grace of God our Father, communion must be reestablished between those who by faith have acknowledged and accepted Jesus Christ as the Lord of mercy who sets men free and unites them in the Spirit of love and truth. For this reason the Jubilee Year, which the Catholic Church has accepted as part of her own custom and tradition, can serve as a most opportune period for spiritual renewal and for the promotion of Christian unity.

.   .   .   .

For our part we would hope that all who come to Rome to see Peter may through us experience in the Holy Year the truth of the words of Saint Leo the Great: " For in the whole Church Peter repeats each day, ' You are Christ the Son of the Living God ', and every tongue which confesses the Lord is inspired by the teaching of this voice. "

.   .   .   .

We implore the Blessed Virgin Mary, the Holy Mother of the Redeemer and of the Church, Mother of grace and of mercy, collaborator of reconciliation and shining example of the new life, to ask her Son to grant to all our brethren and sons and daughters the grace of this Holy Year, to renew and preserve them. To her hands and to her maternal heart we commend the beginning, the development and the conclusion of this most important matter.

Given in Rome, at Saint Peter's, on the twenty-third day of May, the Solemnity of the Ascension of the Lord, in the Year one thousand nine hundred and seventy-four, the eleventh of our Pontificate.

I PAUL
BISHOP OF THE
CATHOLIC CHURCH

The Holy Door
of St. Peter's.

Right: Boniface VIII
proclaims the first
Holy Year (painting
attributed to Giotto).

What is the Holy Year?

Pope Paul VI
concludes the Good
Friday *Via Crucis*
at the Basilica
of Massenzio:
the Holy Year is above all
time of penitence and
reconciliation.

« The Holy Year »—as the Pope explained in giving the announcement of it—« was, in the Biblical tradition, a year of special public life, with abstention from normal work, the retouching of the original distribution of land, the cancelling of current debts, and the liberation of the Hebrew slaves (cf. Lev. 25, 8 ff.).

In the language of Canon Law, the Holy Year is called « jubilee ». In Church History, as everyone knows, the Jubilee was instituted by Pope Boniface VIII in 1300. It consisted of a penitential pilgrimage to the tombs of the Apostles Peter and Paul, in which Dante took part and described the great crowds in Rome in that year in his *Divine Comedy* (Inf. XVIII, 28-33. In the Jubilee Year of 1500, the opening of the Holy Doors of the Basilicas to be visited was added to the ceremonies, not only to facilitate the entrance of the great crowd of penitents, but also to symbolize the easier access to divine mercy by means of obtaining the Holy Year indulgence ». (*From the address given by the Holy Father at the general audience of May 9, 1973, in St. Peter's Basilica*).

Pope Paul VI
opens the Holy Year
in the cathedral of
San Giovanni
in Laterano.

Below: Pope Paul VI gives
the first announcement
of the 1975 Holy Year.

The Holy Father
kisses the Cross in the
Good Friday liturgy.

Below: a historical moment
in the Church.
Bishops of the world
come to the opening
of the Council.

The Jubilee Year 1975

The second Jubilee was announced for the year 1350 by Pope Clement VI with the papal bull « *Unigenitus* » of January 27, 1343. This added the Basilica of St. John Lateran to the two of St. Peter and St. Paul, which had already been designated for obligatory visits by Boniface VIII.

In 1389 Urban VI reduced the interval from one Holy Year to the next from 50 to 33 years in memory of the number of years of Jesus Christ's life, but since Urban died in the meantime, the Jubilee was celebrated the following year (1390) by his successor Boniface IX. Later Nicholas V decided to return to the decree of Clement VI and inaugurated the Holy Year on Christmas Eve of 1449. Paul II with the papal Bull « *Ineffabilis Providentia* » of April 17, 1470, decreed that the Holy Year should be celebrated every 25 years. The Holy Year of 1975, our Holy Year, is the twenty-fifth in history, and it acquires a particular prominence because it follows in time and in spirit the Second Vatican Council.

It is the same pope who is linking the Holy Year to this fundamental moment in the life of the Church. As the recent Council was an extraordinary occasion for renewal and encounter, so also this Jubilee must be distinguished by a great effort towards renewal, reconciliation, and unity.

The 1975 Holy Year searches above all for « the interior renewal of man »—as the Pope has said—« of the man who

Above: the precious graffiti of the Catacombs of San Sebastiano: sign of the ancient veneration of the Apostles.

Below: The Sepulcher of the Apostle Peter on Vatican hill.

thinks, and in thinking has lost the certainty of the Truth; of man who works and in working has realized that he is so bent outside of himself that he no longer hears his own personal inner voice enough; of man that enjoys and has fun and gains from the ways that are supposed to move him to a joyful experience only a feeling of boredom and disappointment ».

Finally, the celebration of this Jubilee is characterized by the fact that, according to the Pope's wish, it began in the local churches on Pentecost, 1973, and will gravitate towards the church in Rome, Mother and Queen of all the Churches.

Below: Pope Paul VI and the Patriarch Atenagora: two great pillars of the Ecumenical Movement.

Indulgences and ecumenism

The essence of the Holy Year consists in the pilgrimage, performed with penitence and with the purpose of gaining the indulgences. Indulgences were often criticized in the course of Church History, above all at the beginning of the XVI century, when Luther began a movement of « protest » that he himself, however, believed was within the Church, neither outside nor less still against the Church.

Since that time many things have changed. The Counter-Reformation clarified the misunderstandings arising from an erroneous interpretation of indulgences, stating precisely that no offering of money has any value for the soul without a severe and truthful pledge to live a Christian life.

If on one hand indulgences are still a reason for dissent among Protestants, on the other hand the Catholic Church,

15

The ecumenical meeting of Pope Paul VI and the Patriarch Atenagora at Jerusalem.

A fraternal meeting of Pope John XXIII with non-Catholic observers at the Council.

thanks to the Ecumenical Movement and above all to the Apostolic Constitution of Paul VI, « *Indulgentiarium Doctrina* » of January I, 1967, has brought the doctrine up to date in an important way on this point, by bringing the indulgence back to its original meaning, which is that of penitence and prayer, putting the accent, as a Protestant brother did at the World Council of Churches in Geneva, on the concept that Jesus Christ is the true and the only plenary indulgence.

From every part of the world the crowds of the faithful are coming together towards the holy city of Rome. This event is a rare and concrete manifestation of that unity, the precious heritage of the Catholic Church, that is actuated and identified in the person of the successor of St. Peter, by the will of God, Bishop of Rome and Head of the Universal Church.

Why Rome was selected by God to be the seat of the Supreme Pontiff is one of His mysteries, which are above all human understanding.

Studies and research have not yet definitively resolved some doubts about the difficult and controversial period of the antipopes. But the care with which the succession of the popes has been handed down through the centuries signifies the exceptional importance of the Apostolic See of Rome. The means of electing the Bishop of Rome has changed in the course of the centuries, but the symbolic thread that binds all of the successors of St. Peter has remained uninterrupted. Here is a list of the succession of the popes. Even during the period of their residence in Avignon they remained popes and also Bishops of Rome.

Pope Paul VI on the path
of ecumenical reconciliation:

Above and *on the right*: Visiting the
Ecumenical Council at Geneva.

Below: with Archbishop
Ramsey, Primate of England.

Below on the right:
at the U.N. The Church
seemed to become in that visit
the visible sacrament of all mankind.

Holy Years

I	- 1300	Pope	Boniface VIII
II	- 1350	Pope	Clement VI
III	- 1390	Pope	Urban VI
		Pope	Boniface IX
IV	- 1400	Pope	Boniface IX
V	- 1425	Pope	Martin V
VI	- 1450	Pope	Nicholas V
VII	- 1475	Pope	Sistus IV
VIII	- 1500	Pope	Alexander VI
IX	- 1525	Pope	Clement VII
X	- 1550	Pope	Julius III
XI	- 1575	Pope	Gregory XIII
XII	- 1600	Pope	Clement VIII
XIII	- 1625	Pope	Urban VIII
XIV	- 1650	Pope	Innocent X
XV	- 1675	Pope	Clement X
XVI	- 1700	Pope	Innocent XII
		Pope	Clement XI
XVII	- 1725	Pope	Benedict XIII
XVIII	- 1750	Pope	Benedict XIV
XIX	- 1775	Pope	Clement XIV
		Pope	Pius VI
XX	- 1825	Pope	Leo XII
XXI	- 1875	Pope	Pius IX
XXII	- 1900	Pope	Leo XIII
XXIII	- 1925	Pope	Pius XI
XXIV	- 1950	Pope	Pius XII
XXV	- 1975	Pope	Paul VI

The regular Holy Years are, therefore, twenty-five. They become twenty-six, if one adds the extraordinary Holy Year celebrated in 1933, proclaimed by Pope Pius X in memory of the thirty-three years in Jesus' life.

URBANO VI   BONIFACIO IX   MARTINO V   NICCOLO' V

CLEMENTE VII   GIULIO III   GREGORIO XIII   CLEMENTE VIII

CLEMENTE X   INNOCENZO XII   CLEMENTE XI   BENEDETTO XIII

PIO VI   LEONE XII   PIO IX   LEONE XIII

PIO XI   PIO XII   PAOLO VI

The four major Basilicas
are the « four sides » of
Christian Rome,
to which the
Catholic world looks as to
the cornerstone of the
universal Church.

The Holy Door

Every Jubilee begins with the solemn opening of the Holy Door. We have known about this door since the XV century.

Above all the door signifies Christ, the Alpha and the Omega, the beginning and the end, Jesus, who defined himself as the *Door*, through which the soul has access to communion with the Father, in order to obtain reconciliation with God.

It is the symbol and the almost tangible certainty that divine mercy is great and open to all those who invoke it with sincerity and a contrite spirit. It means the passing, in the light of Christ, from a life of sin to a life of love and glory. As the Jubilee is inspired by a remembrance of an old custom of the people of Israel, so the Holy Door records the extraordinary event of the crossing of the Red Sea by the Jews, a symbol and foreshadowing of the passage of Christ from death to life.

The Holy Door also signifies the access to the *Confession*, where the remains of the Apostles lie and where the record of their testimony is.

One crosses this door not only to pray at the tombs of the Apostles, but also in order to enter humbly into their spirit, to become one with them in their faith. Lastly, the Holy Door has an ecumenical meaning. It makes us remember that there is only one Flock and one Shepherd, Christ, of whom the Roman Pontiff is the vicar.

The pilgrims, no matter what denomi-

The bronze door
of the ancient basilica
of Saint Paul forged
in Costantinople in 1070
and signed by Staurachio
di Scio—one of
the most outstanding
examples of Byzantine
art in Italy.

The Pope recites the
Angelus with the faithful
every Sunday at noon.

nation they belong to, by crossing this door reaffirm their faith in the Unity, the Universality, and the Apostolicity of the Church. The « creed » that they sing at the tombs of the Apostles is a profound ecclesiastical expression, worthy of the ardent faith of the martyrs and the early Christians, of whom we still have a moving testimony in the catacombs.

In each of the four major Basilicas (St. Peter's, St. John Lateran, St. Paul's, and St. Mary Major) there is a Holy Door to the right of the main entrance. On Christmas Eve the pope goes to the portal of St. Peter's in front of the Holy Door, walled up at the end of the preceding Jubilee. With a silver hammer he hits the door three times while singing the verse « *Aperite mihi portas iustitiae* » (« open to me, doors of justice »). After him the Cardinal Penitentiary knocks at the same door, but only twice.

The wall, having been cut previously, gives way. The penitentiaries wash the threshold, and the pope crosses it first, holding a cross in his right hand a lighted candle in the left. The ceremony is performed in the same way in the other three patriarchial Basilicas, at St. Paul's by the Cardinal Deacon, at St. John Lateran and St. Mary Major by the respective Cardinal archpriests. For the closing of the Holy Door, at the end of the Jubilee, the same ceremony is celebrated inversely. The pope sprinkles a little lime on the threshold three times and puts three stones there. In these stones, the commemorative medals of the Jubilee, coined in the same year, are enclosed. Then the door is walled up until the beginning of the next Jubilee.

Pope Pius XII at the ceremony opening
the 1950 Holy Year.

Pope Pius XII closes the
Holy Door
on Christmas Day, 1950.

PILGRIM'S PRAYERS

Prayers included in the Holy Year liturgy.

PATER NOSTER

Pater noster qui es in Cœlis, sanctificétur nomen tuum: advéniat regnum tuum: fiat volùntas tua, sicut in Cœlo et in terra. Panem nostrum quotidiànum da nobis hòdie, et dimìtte nobis débita nostra, sicut et nos dimìttimus debitòribus nostris; et ne nos indùcas in tentatiònem, sed libera nos a malo. Amen.

CREDO

Credo in unum Deum, Patrem omnipoténtem, factórem cæli et terræ, visibílium ómnium et invisibílium. Et in unum Dóminum Iesum Christum, Fílium Dei unigénitum. Et ex Patre natum ante ómnia saécula. Deum de Deo, lumen de lúmine, Deum verum de Deo vero. Génitum, non factum, consubstatiálem Patri: per quem ómnia facta sunt. Qui propter nos hómines et propter nostram salútem descéndit de cælis. Et incarnátus est de Spíritu Sancto ex María Vírgine: et homo factus est. Crucifíxus étiam pro nobis: sub Póntio Piláto passus, et sepúltus est. Et resurréxit tertia die, secúndum Scriptúras. Et ascéndit in cælum: sedet ad déxtéram Patris. Et íterum ventúrus est cum glóría iudicáre vivos et mórtuos: cuius regni non erit finis. Et in Spíritum Sanctum, Dóminum et vivificántem: qui ex Patre Filióque procédit. Qui cum Patre et Fílio simul adorátur et conglorificátur: qui locútus est per Prophétas. Et unam sanctam cathólicam et apostólicam Ecclésiam. Confíteor unum baptísma in remissiónem peccatórum. Et expécto resurrectiónem mortuórum. Et vitam ventúri saéculi. Amen.

AVE MARIA

Ave Maria, gràtia plena; Dòminus tecum: benedìcta tu in muliéribus, et benedìctus fructus ventris tui, Jesus. Sancta Marìa, Mater Dei, ora pro nobis peccatòribus, nunc et in hora mortis nostræ. Amen.

GLORIA PATRI

Glòria Patri et Fìlio et Spirìtui Sancto, sicut erat in princìpio, et nunc, et semper, et in sæcula sæculòrum. Amen.

PRECES PRO SUMMO PONTIFICE

1.

Sacerdos:

Orémus pro Pontífice nostro Paulo.

Omnes:

Dóminus exáudiat eum
et virtúte corróboret,
ut fratres suos confírmet.

Sacerdos:

Omnípotens et miséricors Deus, qui benigne semper operáris ut possímus implére quæ præcipis: dilectárum tibi óvium adésto Pastóri, et in hunc afféctum dírige cor plebis et præsulis ut nec Pastóri obœdiéntia gregis, nec gregi desit cura Pastóris, quia tui est múneris tuæque virtútis, ut et regéndi obœdiéntes, et probábiles possint esse rectóres.
Per Christum Dóminum nostrum.

R. Amen.

2.

Sacerdos:

Orémus pro Pontífice nostro Paulo.

Omnes:

Dóminus confírmet eum,
et in salútem ómnium géntium
Apostolórum spíritu répleat.

Sacerdos:

Deus qui in apóstoli Petri successióne fámulum tuum Paulum elegísti totíus gregis esse pastórem, supplicántem pópulum intuére propítius, et præsta, ut, qui Christi vices gerit in terris, fratres confírmet, et omnis Ecclésia cum ipso commúnicet in vínculo unitátis, amóris et pacis, quátenus in te, animárum pastóre, omnes veritátem et vitam assequántur ætérnam.
Per Christum Dóminum nostrum.

R. Amen.

3.

Sacerdos:

Orémus pro Pontífice nostro Paulo.

Omnes:

Dóminus consérvet eum,
ut Sancti Spíritus múnere
univérsam Ecclésiam ministrándo gubérnet.

Sacerdos:

Deus qui providéntiæ tuæ consílio super beátum Petrum, céteris Apóstolis præpósitum, Ecclésiam tuam ædificári voluísti, réspice propítius ad papam nostrum Paulum, et concéde, ut, quem Petri constituísti successórem, pópulo tuo visíbile sit unitátis fidei et communiónis princípium et fundaméntum. Per Christum Dóminum nostrum.

R. Amen.

4.

Sacerdos:

Orémus pro Pontífice nostro Paulo.

Omnes:

Dóminus servet eum in lumen gentium,
et regat eum in Ecclésiæ sanctitátem.

Sacerdos:

Da quæsumus, Dómine, pacem Ecclésiæ tuæ cui fámulum tuum Paulum præésse voluísti, ut in uno eodémque spíritu sit tibi grata devótio et plebis et præsulis, et increméntum gregis atque salúbritas gáudium sit et coróna Pastóris. Per Christum Dóminum nostrum.

R. Amen.

5.

Sacerdos:

Orémus pro Pontífice nostro Paulo.

Omnes:

Dóminus consérvet eum,
et incólumem custódiat Ecclésiæ suæ,

ad regéndum pópulum sanctum Dei.

Sacerdos:

Deus pastor ætérne fidélium, qui Ecclésiæ tuæ multíplici dispensatióne præes et amóre domináris, da, quæsumus, fámulo tuo Paulo, quem plebi tuæ præfecísti, ut gregi, cuius est pastor, Christi vice præsídeat, et fidélis sit doctrínæ magíster, sacri cultus sacérdos et gubernatiónis miníster. Per Christum Dóminum nostrum.

R. Amen.

6.

Sacerdos:

Orémus pro Pontífice nostro Paulo.

Omnes:

Dóminus consérvet eum, et vivíficet eum,
et beátum fáciat eum in terra,
et non tradat eum in ánimam inimicórum eius.

Sacerdos:

Deus, ómnium fidélium pastor et rector, fámulum tuum Paulum, quem pastórem Ecclésiæ tuæ præésse voluísti, propítius réspice; da ei, quæsumus, verbo et exémplo, quibus præest profícere, ut ad vitam, una cum grege sibi crédito, pervéniat sempitérnam. Per Christum Dóminum nostrum.

R. Amen.

PRAYER FOR THE HOLY YEAR

Lord God and Father, in the death and resurrection of Jesus Christ your Son you willed to reconcile all mankind to yourself and so to reconcile men with each other in peace. Hear the prayer of your people in this year of grace and salvation. R.

In prayer with a group or community, the normal invocations could be used for the people's response e.g. v. Lord, in your mercy, R. Hear our prayer, *or:* v. Lord, hear us, R. Lord, graciously hear us, *or:* v. Lord, have mercy, R. Lord, have mercy.

Let your Spirit of life and holiness renew us, in the depths of our being: unite us throughout our life to the risen Christ: for he is our brother and Saviour. R.

With all Christians we seek to follow the way of the Gospel. Keep us faithful to the teaching of the Church and alive to the needs of our brothers. Give us strength to work for reconciliation, unity and peace. R.

May those who seek the God they do not yet know discover in you the source of light and hope: may those who work for others find strength in you: may those who know you seek even further and experience the depths of your love. R.

Forgive us our sins: deepen our faith: kindle our hope, and enliven our hearts with love for our brothers. May we walk in the footsteps of Christ as your beloved sons and daughters. R.

With the help of Mary, our Mother, may your Church be the sign and sacrament of salvation for all men: that the world may believe in your love and your truth. R.

Father, of your great goodness, hear in the words of your people the prayer of the Spirit to the praise of your glory and the salvation of men. Through Jesus Christ your Son our Lord, the Way, the Truth and the Life, for ever and ever.

R. Amen.

In private prayer the respones (R) after each invocation is omitted and the final prayer is completely omitted. Instead of the final prayer, the simple conclusion: Throught Christ our Lord. Amen.

A VISIT
TO CHRISTIAN ROME

This guidebook has been conceived especially as a « vademecum » for the pilgrim, with the purpose of introducing him to Christian Rome, consecrated by the presence of the Apostles and the Martyrs.

It will also indicate, of course, the most important aspects of ancient and modern Rome.

The « Quo Vadis? » church where St. Peter is said to have met Christ

On the left: St. Peter martyrdom

Below: the basilica of St. Peter the « heart » of Christian Rome

A graffito in the catacombs of S. Sebastiano, left by an early Christian who had come tò venerate the Apostles.

Right: St. Paul's martyrdom.

Via Appia (The Appian Way)

The Old Appian Way was the most important of the consular roads that radiated from Rome towards the distant provinces of the Empire. Built by Appius Claudius, censor in 213 B.C., it connected Rome with Capua and later with Benevento, Brindisi, and Taranto. This road has a prominent significance for Christian Rome too, because it was the road by which the Apostles Peter and Paul, having probably docked at Pozzuoli, came to Rome, thus making this city, by divine will, the center of Christianity. Near the city the road was flanked by funeral monuments, because it was forbidden by law to bury the dead inside the city. About eight hundred meters from the Porta Appia, later called the Porta di San Sebastiano, the church of « QUO VADIS? » is found on the left. This church was erected on the spot where Jesus appeared to St. Peter, who, terrified by the fierce persecution of the Emperor Nero, was fleeing from Rome. Peter asked him, « *Domine, quo vadis?* » (Lord, where are you going?). And the Lord answered him, « I am going to Rome to be crucified a second time ». The Apostle, repentant, went back into the city, where he was imprisoned and martyred.

On the left:
picturesque view
of the Via Appia,
showing ruins of monumental tombs.

A beautiful tomb
on the Via Appia.

The Tomb of
Cecilia Metella.

Two views of the
Via Appia.
This consular road,

still intact in many
sections, led the Apostles
Peter and Paul to Rome.

The catacombs

The catacombs are underground tunnels in the form of a labyrinth many miles long. In the beginning they were Christian cemeteries; later they were places of refuge and prayer. Like the pagan tombs the catacombs were outside the city, along the great consular roads. The word « catacomb » dates from the 1st century A.D., and it originally meant « near the hole ». Later the word « catacomb » was to become one of the most fascinating and revered words in the Christian world, since it represents the testimony of the sufferings and the

Most of the catacombs are found at the beginning of the Via Appia. The tombs of the dead, in fact, were placed along the roads. Some, before becoming Christian cemeteries, were pagan burial grounds. These views show the four most important catacombs: of Priscilla of Domitilla, of San Callisto and of San Sebastiano.

glory of the martyrs, united with the silent and suffering life of the early Christian community.

About forty catacombs are counted in Rome, but it is thought that there are actually many more. Most of them are located on the sides of the first part of the Via Appia (San Sebastiano, Domitilla, San Callisto). This is because the terrain in that part of the city had layers of tufa of vulcanic origin which were very resistant to landslides. The tombs were dug along the sides of the tunnels and could contain up to three bodies. They were closed with slabs of stone or marble, on which were written the name of the deceased and an invocation.

The paintings that decorated them are still of great interest. They are the oldest example of Christian art that we have. The most common symbols are the *Fish*, the *Dove*, the *Good Shepherd*; and there are scenes from the *Old* and *New Testaments*, like, for example the episode of the Prophet Jonah and the « *fractio panis* ».

From the time of the Edict of Milan (March, 313 A.D.), the catacombs were gradually abandoned as burial places, and they became places of pilgrimage. At the beginning of the barbarian invasions the popes ordered the bodies of the martyrs to be transferred to the city churches so that they would not be profaned. Thus the catacombs were completely forgotten. They were rediscovered by chance in 1587 by a peasant, who, digging for pozzolana, fell into a tunnel lined with tombs.

The most important catacombs

The catacombs considered to be among the most important are those of San Sebastiano, San Callisto, Domitilla, and Priscilla, both because they are bound up with particular recollections of martyrs and because of their intrinsic artistic value.

The pilgrim is able to visit the catacombs easier with the guide service supplied for all the catacombs.

SAN SEBASTIANO: The Basilica of San Sebastiano (St. Sebastian), dedicated at first to the Holy Apostles Peter and Paul, together with the catacombs of the same name, constitutes one of the most important Christian treasures.

Today it seems historically certain that the martyrdom of both Peter and Paul took place under the same emperor (Nero) in 64 A.D., but not on the same day, as a legend would have us believe, according to which the two Apostles met on the way to their places of martyrdom and gave each other an embrace of peace as if to pardon each other for the rivalry they had had in life. It is instead very likely that St. Peter found himself mixed up in the mass of Christians accused of being responsible for the burning of Rome. Paul on the other hand, being *civis romanus*—that is, a citizen of Rome— was executed later, with the privilege of being beheaded, while Peter was crucified.

The bones of the two Apostles, during the persecution under Valerian, found refuge at the third milestone of the Via Appia in the place called *Catacumbas*, where later the emperor Constantine had the *Basilica Apostolorum* erected. This remained the name of the church until the high Middle Ages when the cult of St. Sebastian passed from the catacombs underneath to the basilica above.

St. Sebastian was one of the most glorious martyrs of the terrible persecution under Diocletian that served only to re-invigorate Christianity. The figure of St. Sebastian became very popular in the plague that devastated Rome in 680 A.D. The catacombs, both for the memory of the Apostles and the veneration of the martyr Sebastian, were a favorite place of pilgrimage for saints. We will mention Gregory the Great, Brigid, Catherine, Charles Borromeo, Philip Neri, Pius V, and still others.

Above: one of the most picturesque galleries of the catacombs of Domitilla.

The pilgrim comes out from the visit to these catacombs with a strong feeling of nostalgia for those times in which the faith, if it was often the cause of martyrdom, was always a reason for glory.

The symbols painted on the walls are those common to the other catacombs; *The Man in Prayer, The Little Sheep,* the *Tree,* the *Anchor,* and above all the *Fish,* the chief emblem of faith in Christ the Saviour.

These catacombs were certainly a pagan burial ground before becoming a Christian cemetery. They consist of three super-imposed levels that extend for miles. The level which is usually shown to visitors is the middle one because it is the best preserved. In fact it must be remembered that these catacombs have suffered great damage due to man and the passage of time because

they were the only ones accessible during the entire Middle Ages.

The pilgrim can observe with veneration the greetings to and the invocations of the Apostles Peter and Paul, left on the walls by the early Christians. Today these graffiti are an important historical document confirming the presence and the martyrdom of the Apostles at Rome.

Below: Chapel in the catacombs of San Sebastiano.

SAN CALLISTO (*St. Callixtus*): The catacombs owe their name to the deacon Callixtus, the head of the cemetery who later became pope and who made these catacombs the official tomb of the bishops of Rome.

The monuments that merit particular mention are the *Cripta dei Papi* (Crypt of the Popes), the *Cripta dei Santi Sisto e Cecilia* (Crypt of Sts. Sixtus and Cecilia) with frescoes representing *Sant'Urbino*, the *Testa del Salvatore* (Saviour's Head), *St. Cecilia*; the five *Cubicoli dei Sacramenti* with frescoes symbolic of Baptism, Penance, and the Eucharist; the *Cripta di Papa Eusebio* (Pope Eusebius), and finally the *Tomba di Papa Cornelio* (tomb of Pope Cornelius) with Byzantine Paintings and the Latin inscription with the title of MARTYR.

DOMITILLA: From the Via Appia we reach Via delle Sette Chiese that leads to the Catacombs of Domitilla, which are noted both for the richness of their paintings and for the testimony they give to the fact that already by the end of the 1st century, the Christian religion had penetrated all of the social classes, even touching the imperial family. It has been proved historically that these catacombs were developed on a pre-existing cemetery of the « Flavi »

Catacombs of Domitilla:
Madonna with Child.

Catacombs of
San Sebastiano:
the three mausoleums.

and near a *praedium* of Domitilla, who was a niece of the Emperor Domiziano and a convinced follower of Christianity. Later she was banished and martyred on the island of Ponza .

The development of the catacombs was horizontal rather than vertical. We find several levels only in some places. The terrain had, in fact, less firm levels of tufa. One of the motives that contributed to the development of the cemetery of Domitilla was the veneration of the martyrs Nereo and Achilleo, who were buried there.

At the entrance of the catacomb the visitor finds himself in front of a magnificent basilica with three naves. It is dedicated to the two martyrs, who tradition tells us were soldiers before being converted to Christianity. They were entrusted by the courts with an ugly task: that of torturing and killing.

PRISCILLA: Other catacombs of great historical and artistic interest are those of Priscilla on Via Salaria.

These catacombs constitute one of the oldest Christian cemeteries in Rome. Certainly their underground burial chambers date from the first part of the II century A.D. Their foundress was Priscilla, who belonged to a senatorial family. She thought of creating this underground burial chamber for the burial of members of her family and some of the faithful of the Christian community in Rome.

The tunnels of the cemetery are developed on two main levels, the higher of which is the older. Worthy of notice are the cubicle of the *Velatia*, on the back wall of which is painted the *Orante*; and the arch of the Greek Chapel with the beautiful painting of the *Frac-*

Above: Sarcaphagus with
Biblical scenes
(4th century) in the
catacombs of
San Callisto.

Below: left, detail of the *Orante*
in the catacombs of Priscilla.
Right: a Third Century
gallery in the catacombs
of San Callisto.

tio Panis and the Basilica of Papa Silvestro (Pope Sylvester), one of the Bishops of Rome who chose to be buried here. In these catacombs too there are many paintings of the Madonna, a very ancient sign of the cult of the Mother of God among the early Christians.

Worthy of note among the many other catacombs are the ones in the description that follows.

SAN PANCRAZIO: This was dug in a garden that belonged to a lady called *Octavilla.* The young boy Pancrazio, martyred during the persecution of Valerian, was buried here. Only a few of the tunnels can be visited. The Basilica of San Pancrazio was constructed in the VII century by Onorius I. The medieval façade was restored in the XVIII century. In the interior, which has three naves, the pilasters were substituted for the original columns in the first part of the XVII century. Alexander VII had the church embellished at the same time. Also of the same epoch are the eight bas-reliefs in stucco that adorn the side walls: *St. John of the Cross,* the *Holy Prophet Elias, St. John the Baptist, St. Calepodius, St. Julius the Senator, Sts. Processus and Martignanus, Pope St. Felice,* and *St. Pancrazio.* The relics of the martyr are contained under the altar.

SANTA AGNESE (*St. Agnes*): This is a catacomb that was dug before the burial of the body of the martyr (258 A.D.) from whom it takes its name. It is divided into two zones. That to the left dates from before the III century. That to the right, composed of two

Above: catacomb of Domitilla, Galleria dei Flavi.

Right: The Greek Chapel in the catacomb of Priscilla.

Below: an impressive gallery in the catacomb of Priscilla.

groups of tunnels, dates from the IV century.

We have access to the catacomb from the Basilica of St. Agnes, erected in 324 by Constance, the daughter of Constantine, on the spot where the young saint was martyred and buried. The basilica was restored under the pontificate of Simmacus and reconstructed by Onorius I. There have been later restorations, the most recent owing to Pius IX (1856). The interior, which conserves the characteristics of the ancient Christian churches, is divided into three naves with sixteen columns. In the VII century the « matroneo » (the part of the church reserved for the women) was added. There is a statue of the saint on the high altar. This is an old Roman statue completed in the baroque period. Under the altar there are the remains of St. Agnes and those of another saint, Emerenziana. The mosaic of the apse is in Byzantine style, of the time of Onorius I, who is represented in it, along with Simmacus and St. Agnes.

Above: the Fourth Century subterranean basilica in the catacombs of Santa Domitilla.

CIRIACA: This catacomb is found under the Basilica of San Lorenzo Fuori le Mura (St. Laurence Outside the Walls). It was dug on the land belonging to a matron named Ciriaca, and it became important when the martyr St. Laurence was buried there. The cemetery occupied the area on which the Basilica was later erected, and it extended under the nearby hill also. It was damaged in part by construction work on the present city cemetery of Verano. In the part still visible there are preserved some paintings, among which is the parable of the *Vergini*

Below: the tricora of San Sisto (4th century) in the catacombs of San Callisto.

Prudenti e delle Vergini stolte (The Wise and Foolish Virgins). This catacomb can be visited only with special permission.

PRETESTATO: The entrance is almost directly opposite the cemetery of Callisto. It was already in existence in the II century when the martyr Gennaro (Januarius), oldest son of Santa Felicita (162 A.D.), was buried here. In 1830 a cubicle with paintings of the II century was discovered here. The crypt of San Gennaro is adorned with valuable paintings.

The underground burial place of *Vibio* makes up a part of this cemetery. (It can be visited only by special permission).

DEI GIORDANI: These are the deepest catacombs of Rome and are composed of five levels. The married couple, Chrysantus and Daria, were buried here in a large sandstone area. In the story of their martyrdom it is told that some Christians, gathered together to pray at their tombs, were buried alive under a pile of rocks thrown by their persecutors. Three of the seven sons of Santa Felicita were buried here, namely Martial, Vitale, and Alexander. Interesting paintings are to be found here. (Special permission is required to see them).

SANTA FELICITA (*St. Felicitas*): These catacombs take their name from a martyr of the persecution of Marcus Aurelius (162 A.D.) who was buried here together with Silanus, the youngest of her sons. The place of burial of St. Felicitas was re-discovered in the excavations of 1885. At the foot of the hill there is a little underground basilica with the remains of a Byzantine painting representing the Bust of the Saviour with St. Felicitas and her children. The cemetery is very devastated. (It is difficult to see these catacombs and special permission is required).

The « four-sided » Christian in the Eternal City

We suggest that the pilgrim imagine Christian Rome as being symbolically constructed on a quadrilateral constituted by the four major Basilicas, that, together with the catacombs, are the crossroads of the expectations and the aspirations of all Christian peoples.

Catacomb of San Callisto: a gallery (third century).

Catacombs of Priscilla: the *Fractio Panis*, one of the most beautiful paintings in the catacombs.

St. Peter's Basilica and the See of the Vicar of Christ.

Having crossed the Tiber, at the beginning of Via della Conciliazione, the pilgrim finds in front of him the unique view of the great Basilica of San Pietro (St. Peter's Basilica), with the massive colonnade that wants to symbolically embrace the Catholic World and invite the faithful to gather together at the tomb of the Prince of the Apostles. Near the greatest church in Christendom the pope, the successor of St. Peter, has his usual residence, and as the successor of St. Peter, he is also Bishop of Rome and Supreme Pontiff of the Universal Church.

The first church was constructed by Constantine on the circus of Nero, where the Apostle suffered martyrdom. His body was buried in the little Christian cemetery that was near the circus, on the slopes of Vatican Hill.

Basilica of St. Peter:
detail of the Pietà
by Michelangelo;
statue of the Apostle Peter
with pontifical robes;
the Holy Door.

THE BASILICA: The church that Constantine had built, in 326 A.D. upon request of Pope Sylvester I, was erected on the spot of the little Oratory which Bishop Anacletus had built on the tomb of the martyr in 90 A.D. It had five naves that all rested on the walls of the circus of Nero. Rich in countless art treasures and full of the tombs of popes and emperors, it was ruined by the course of time. Nothing remains of this old Basilica.

The stupendous vision that Piazza San Pietro (St. Peter's square) offers today is due chiefly to the genius of Miche-

langelo and Bernini. 284 columns in four rows and 88 pilasters compose the majestic colonnade, covered by a loggia on which there are 140 statues of saints. The square measures 240 meters in length and 200 meters in width.

At the center rises the obelisk that the Emperor Caligula had brought from Heliopolis and that Nero had placed in the Circus Maximus. Its placement, by order of Sixtus V, was carried out by Domenico Fontana in 1586 and became legendary because of the enormous difficulties encountered. 800 men and 150 horses were needed. On both sides between the baroque fountains and the obelisk, two circular stones have been inserted in the pavement. These stones mark the points from which we can observe, with marvelous optical effect, the colonnade on only one circle of columns.

The first stone of the new church was put into position by Pope Julius II on April 18, 1506. The consecration of the Basilica was celebrated by Pope Urban VIII on November 18, 1626. In the hundred and twenty years that were needed to construct the Basilica the greatest artists of the time brought their genius to bear on it: from Bramante, the first architect, to Raphael, from Giuliano and Antonio da Sangallo to Baldassarre Peruzzi, from Michelangelo, who revised Bramante's original project, to Vignola, from Ligorio to Della Porta to Domenico Fontana to Carlo Maderno. The great façade, erected by Maderno in 1612, is preceded by a set of wide stairs flanked by statues of Peter and Paul. The façade is 115 meters long and 46 meters high, and it has eight columns with four pilasters and nine large windows. At the center there

Above: St. Peter's throne by Bernini.

Michelangelo's magnificent dome.

Below: the papal altar with baldachin by Bernini.

is the balcony for the solemn benedictions *Urbi et Orbi* (to the city and the world) and for the announcement of the name of the new pope elected in the Conclave.

Five entrances lead to the portal. At the extreme right is the statue of *Constantine* by Bernini; at the extreme left the statue of *Charlemagne* by Cornacchini.

Above the central entrance is the famous mosaic the *Navicella* (The Little Boat) by Giotto, brought from the old Basilica. The eleven Apostles are on board the ship, symbol of the Church Militant, that in the tempestuous sea of the centuries follows the route accompanied by the invisible presence of Christ.

There are five doors leading into the Basilica, of which the last to the right is the *Holy Door*, that remains open for entire duration of the Jubilee. The central door, the work of Filarete, which was also in the old Basilica, is composed of six panels representing the *Saviour*, the *Virgin, St. Peter, St. Paul*, and *Scenes of the trial and beheading of Paul and his appearance to Plautilla*, and the *Martyrdom of St. Peter*.

Upon entering, the extraordinary architectural harmony does not give, at first sight, an exact idea of the dimensions of the immense Basilica. Bramante's conception of the church in the form of a Greek cross—effected by Michelangelo—overhung by the enormous dome, was partially modified by Maderno, who made the central nave longer. The plan that resulted from this—in the form of a Latin Cross—has three naves. The ceiling of gilded caissons is 44 meters high, while under the dome the height reaches 120 meters.

Above: the basilica of St. Peter seen from the Vatican gardens

Above: the central nave designed by Michelangelo.

Below: detail of Bernini's colonnade.

On the floor in front of the central door there is a porphyry disk which commemorates the spot on which Charlemagne and the other emperors of the Holy Roman Empire knelt down to receive the crown and the investiture from the pope. On the floor of the entire central nave the length of the largest basilica in the world, after that of St. Peter's (186.36 meters), is measured.

Four great arches on Corinthian pilasters make up the central nave, that together with the ceiling and the plan of the dome bear the mark of the genius of Michelangelo.

In the niches there are statues of the holy founders of religious orders. In front of the last pilaster to the right is the bronze statue of St. Peter that dates from 1200 and is attributed to Arnolfo di Cambio. The right foot, consumed by kisses, is the testimony of the contless throngs of pilgrims who for centuries have come to venerate the tomb of the Apostle.

The dome, supported by four enormous pilasters, has a diameter of 42 meters and gives light to the church by means of 16 open windows in the drum. Under the dome there is the bronze baldachino by Bernini which was constructed in 1633 for Urban VII. It overhangs the *Papal Altar*. This altar, so named because only the pope can celebrate the sacred liturgy at it, faces the *Confessione*, the work of Maderno, under which is found the tomb of the Apostle Peter. The altar, together with the tomb of the Apostle, signifies the unity of the local churches in the Universal Church. The statue of Pius VI, in prayer before the remains of the Apostle, is the work of Canova.

The pilasters that support the dome are adorned with niches containing the statues of Longinus, Saint Helena, St. Veronica, and St. Andrew. In the back of the apse the four bronze statues of Saint Ambrose, St. Augustine, St. Athanasius, and St. John Chrysostom support the *Cattedra* (the Chair), the work of Bernini, that contains the *Sedia Lignea* (Wooden Chair) on which, according to tradition, St. Peter sat.

The right nave begins with the *Chapel* called the *Pietà* because it contains the stupendous sculpture by Michelangelo, that represents the inert body of Christ in the lap of the Madonna. It is the only work of the Florentine master that bears his signature, engraved on the band that crosses the breast of the Madonna diagonally.

Passing the chapel we come on the left to the monument to Queen Christina of Sweden, the work of Carlo Fontana. The monument to Leo XII is on the door of the *Cappella del Crocefisso* (Chapel of the Crucifix) by Bernini, where an ancient wooden crucifix by Pietro Cavallini is venerated. The *Cappella di San Sebastiano* (Chapel of St. Sebastian) follows, where there are the monuments to *Pius XI* and *Pius XII*. Proceeding to the right we fiind the tomb of *Innocent XII*, with the allegorical statues of Charity and Justice. Opposite there is the monument to the *Countess Matilda of Canossa* by Bernini. The *Cappella del Sacramento* (Chapel of the Blessed Sacrament) follows. Its grating was designed by Borromini and its bronze tabernacle by Bernini. Coming out of the chapel we see to the right the monument of *Gregory XIII*. A little further on there is the monument to *Gregory XIV* on

The Basilica seen from Via della Conciliazione.

Left: interior of Michelangelo's dome.

The Pope speaks to pilgrims from the window of the Palazzo Apostolico.

The tomb of Pope
Innocent III
by Pollaiolo.

The bronze statue
of Pope Urbano VIII
by Bernini.

the left. To the right there is the
entrance to the *Cappella Gregoriana*
(Gregorian Chapel) by Giacomo Della
Porta. It was designed by Michelangelo. As we continue to the right there
is the monument to *Benedict XIV* by
Bracci. Then we enter the right transept, which was the site of the First
Vatican Council in 1869. Above the
altars there are the three mosaics of *St.
Venceslaos, Sts. Processus and Martignanus,* and *St. Erasmus.* Passing on
to the *Cappella di San Michele* (Chapel
of St. Michael) we see the monument
to *Clement XIII* by Canova. In the
Cappella di Can Michele above the
altar there is a copy in mosaic of a
St. Michael by Guido Reni. Beyond
the chapel, in the passageway that leads
to the tribune, there is the tomb of
Clement X. Proceeding beyond the tribune and the apse we can admire to
the right the sumptuous tomb of *Alexander VIII,* the work of various artists from a design of Arrigo di San
Martino. Above the altar of the *Cappella della Colonna* (Chapel of the Columns) there is the great bas-relief in
marble of the *meeting of Leo I with
Attila* by Alessandro Algardi. In the
passageway to the left transept there is
the *tomb of Alexander VII* by Bernini
Above the central altar of the left
transept we see the mosaic *Crucifixion
of St. Peter* by Guido Reni.
Above the entrance to the sacresty there
is the monument to *Pius VIII.* Then
we enter the *Cappella Clementina* (Cle
mentine Chapel) by Della Porta. The
altar to the right is dedicated to *St
Gregory the Great* and contains the
relics of that pope. Opposite there is
the tomb of *Pius VII.*
Thus we come to the left nave, facing

which, on the pilaster, is the mosaic copy of the *Transfiguration* by Raphael. On the right side of the nave there is the monument to *Leo XI* by Algardi. Opposite this, there is the monument to *Innocent XI*. Then follows: the *Cappella del Coro* (Chapel of the Chorus) closed by gratings and officiated by the Basilica Chapter; the monument to *Pius X*, and to the left the tomb of *Innocent VIII* in bronze, the work of Pollaiolo; and the *Cappella della Presentazione* (Chapel of the Presentation) with the monument to *Benedict XV* of the presbytery and the monument to *John XXIII*, the work of Emilio Greco. Continuing, we come to the Chapel of the *Fonte Battesimale* (Baptismal Font) made of an ancient sarcophagus of red porphyry.

SACRESTY AND TREASURE: The door, that is found under the monument to *Pius VIII*, leads to the Sacresty and the Treasure. A vestibule with columns leads into the octagonal sacresty. On the left we enter the sacresty of the Canonicals, where there is a *Madonna* by Giulio Romano. On the right we enter the sacresty of the *Beneficed Priests*, in which is kept the famous *Ciborium* by Donatello. From here we pass into the rooms where the treasure is kept, a matchless collection of precious objects gathered together over the centuries. The following objects are of particular note: the *Cross of Byzantium* by Giustino (VI century), the famous *Dalmatica said to be of Charlemagne*, the *Chasuble* of Julius II, two *Candelabra* by Pollaiolo, the *Byzantine Crosses of Justin II*, the *Candelabra* by Benvenuto Cellini.

The tomb of Pope Clement XIII carved by Canova.

Detail of the Porta di San Pietro.

PLAN OF
ST. PETER'S BASILICA

1. Atrium
2. Door of the Dead
3. Central door of the Filarete
4. Holy Door
5. Central Nave
6. Chapel of the Pietà
7. Tomb of Leo XII
8. Tomb of Christina of Sweden
9. Tomb of Pius XI
10. Chapel of St. Sebastian
11. Tomb of Pius XII
12. Tomb of Innocent XII
13. Tomb of the Countess
14. Chapel Holy Sacrament
15. Tomb of Gregory XIII
16. Tomb of Gregory XIV
17. Tomb of Gregory XVI
18. Gregorian Chapel
19. Altar. Madonna del Soccorso
20. Altar. St. Jerome
21. Altar. St. Basil
22. Tomb. Benedict XIV
23. Right Transept
24. Altar. St. Wenceslaus
25. Altar. SS. Processo
    and Martiniano
26. Altar. St. Erasmus
27. Altar of the « Navicella »
28. Tomb. Clement XIII
29. Altar. St. Michael, Archangel
30. Altar. St. Petronilla
31. Altar. St. Peter raising Tabitha
32. Tomb. Clement X
33. Nave of the Cathedra
34. Tomb. Urban VIII
35. St. Peter's Cathedra
36. Tomb. Paul III
37. Tomb. Alexander VIII
38. Altar. St. Peter healing
    the paralytic
39. Chapel of the Madonna
    of the Colonna
40. Altar. St. Leo Magno
41. Altar. Madonna della Colonna
42. Tomb. Alexander VII
43. Altar of the Sacred Heart
44. Left Transept
45. Altar. St. Thomas
46. Altar. St. Joseph
47. Altar. Crucifixion of St. Peter
48. Statue. St. Veronica
49. Statue. St. Helen
50. Statue. St. Longino
51. Statue. St. Peter
52. Confession and Papal Altar
53. Statue. St. Andrew
    (grotto entrance)
54. Altar of the « Bugia »
55. Tomb. Pius VIII
    (sacristy entrance)
56. Clementine Chapel
57. Altar. St. Gregory
58. Tomb. Pius VII
59. Altar. Transfiguration
60. Tomb. Leo XI
61. Tomb. Innocent XI
62. Chapel of the Chorus
63. Altar. B. V. Immacolata
64. Tomb. Pius X
65. Tomb. Innocent VIII
66. Tomb. John XXIII
67. Chapel. Presentation
    of the Virgin
68. Tomb. Benedict XV
69. Tomb. M. Clementina
    Sobiesky
70. Tomb of the Stuarts
71. Baptistery
72. Arch of the Bells
73. Mosaic of the « Navicella »

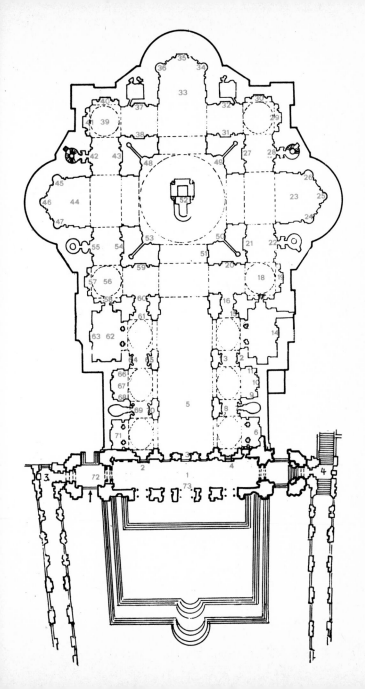

THE DOME: The entrance to the dome is between the first and second chapels of the left nave. We can go up, either in the elevator or by climbing the spiral stairs of 537 steps, to the first terraced roof that covers the Basilica. From here the dome shows its magnificence even more. From the terraced roof two staircases lead to the drum of the dome, that is 53 meters in height. By climbing a succession of stairways we arrive at the balcony of the lantern, 120 meters high, from where we enjoy a stupendous panorama. The ball, to which we have access by a very steep staircase, can hold a dozen people.

THE VATICAN GROTTOES: Rational research, together with vast and methodical archaeological excavations, permitted a few years ago the recognition of the first traces of Christianity and the records of the Apostles, among the first that of the *Fisherman of Galilee*, called by Christ to lead the Church. The Vatican Grottoes were made by a drop of about three meters from the floor of the present Basilica to that, underneath, of the ancient Basilica of Constantine.

Above: the Porta Central of Vatican Cit protected by th Swiss Guard

Their construction was begun by Gregory XIII; those called the *Old Grottoes* comprise the crypt, that has three naves with cross-vaulting, where there are the tombs of *Boniface VIII, Nicholas III*, the Emperor *Otto II*, and *Gregory V*.

The *New Grottoes*, constructed by Clement VIII, continue in the direction of the dome, under the cross-piece, and develop in the form of a semi-circle around the *CAPPELLA DI SAN PIETRO* (*The Chapel of St. Peter*), raised over the tomb of the Apostle. In this place the works ordered by Pius XII

certified the existence of the pagan and Christian necropolis of the II-III centuries and the presence of *Peter's tomb*. Opposite the tomb of the Apostle we find that of *Pius XII*, and further a head that of *John XXIII*.

Vatican city

The « Lateran Pact » of 1929, even if it changed the juridical and geographical configuration of the ancient States of the Church, reaffirmed the inalienable right of the Holy See to be an unsubstitutionable member of the international community. The little nation that is now Vatican City guarantees the Holy See the necessary independence from every political power, an independence that is necessary in order to fulfill its mission as the central organ of the Catholic Church.

From this center, by virtue of the mandate received from Christ and its unique position in history, the pope continues to fulfill his universal ministry in the service of the peoples. Toward this universal homeland of the spirit that is Vatican City, although very small in geographical area (0.440 kilometers in area), the weak and the powerful turn their faces as if to an island of peace and human brotherhood.

In the city's perimeter there are, besides St. Peter's Basilica, the Palazzo Apostolico, the usual residence of the Holy Father, the Palazzo del Governatorato, the Palazzo della Radio Vaticana that, with its broadcasts in thirty three languages, is one of the most powerful transmitting stations in the world in the service of religion and peace. There are also the buildings of the Library,

Below: a view of the Piazza of St. Peter seen from the Dome.

59

MAP OF VATICAN CITY

1 Via S. Anna
2 Via del Pellegrino
3 Via del Belvedere
4 Via della Tipografia
5 Via della Posta
6 Via S. Pio X
7 Salita ai Giardini
8 Stradone ai Giardini
9 Rampa dell'Archeologia
10 Via del Governatorato
11 Via delle Fondamenta
12 Vicolo del Perugino
13 Via S. Egidio
14 Via del Mosaico
15 Viale dell'Osservatorio
16 Via del Collegio Etiopico
17 Viale Guglielmo Marconi
18 Viale della Zitella
19 Viale del Bosco
20 Viale del Giardino Quadrato
21 Bastione dell'Eliporto
22 Viale degli Ulivi
23 Via Nostra Signora
   di Guadalupe
24 Viale Pio XII
25 Bastioni di S. Giovanni
26 Via Pio XI
27 Viale Benedetto XV
28 Vico S. Venerio
29 Viale della Radio
30 Bastione di Maestro
31 Viale Pio IX
32 Viale dello Sport
33 Viale S. Benedetto
34 Viale Leone XIII
35 Viale S. Marco
36 Viale dell'Aquilone
37 Viale Gregorio XVI
38 Viale della Galea
39 Viale della Grotta di Lourdes

40 Viale dell'Accademia delle
   Scienze
41 Via S. Luca
A Piazza S. Pietro
B Largo S. Martino
C Piazza del Forno
D Largo Pier Luigi da Palestrina
E Piazza del Governatorato
F Piazzale della Stazione
G Largo S. Stefano degli Abissini
H Piazza S. Marta
I Largo Braschi
L Largo della Sagrestia
M Piazza dei Protomartiri Romani
N Largo Giovanni XXIII
O Largo Capanna Cinese
P Piazzale della Grotta di Lourdes
Q Largo Madonna della Guardia
R Piazzale S. Chiara
S Largo della Radio
T Piazzale della Galea
U Piazzale del Collegio Etiopico
V Largo S. Matteo
W Largo S. Giuseppe Artigiano
Y Largo S. Giovanni Bosco
Z Largo Fontana del Sacramento
a Cortile dell'Olmo
b Cortile del Maggiordomo
c Cortile Sisto V
d Cortile S. Damaso
e Cortile del Maresciallo
f Cortile dei Pappagalli
g Cortile Borgia
h Cortile della Sentinella
i Cortile del Belvedere
l Cortile della Biblioteca
m Cortile della Pigna
n Cortile delle Corazze
o Cortile del Triangolo
p Cortile S. Michele Arcangelo

the Hall of Records, the Museums, the ancient and modern Picture Galleries, and the new Hall for Audiences.
A large area of the Vatican is covered with marvelous gardens that can be visited with the required permission.

The Vatican Museums

The first papal museums and galleries were begun by the wish of Clement XIV (1769-1774) and that of Pius VI (1775-1799). From these two popes the museum took its name: « Museo Pio Clementino ». Between 1800 and 1823 Pius VII enlarged the museums and added the Museo Chiaramonti, the Galleria Lapidaria, and the Braccio Nuovo. In 1836 Gregory XVI founded the Museo Etrusco with archeological finds from southern Etruria, and in 1839 he founded the Museo Egizio with monuments and curios brought from Egypt or taken from the Museo Capitolino or from other collections.
Pope John XXIII transferred the Museo Profano Lateranense from the Lateran Palaces to the Vatican Museums, putting it into a new building (opened to the public in 1970). To this museum Pius IX had added, in 1854, the Museo Cristiano, including sculpture, sarcophagi, and ancient inscriptions, besides numerous pieces coming from the excavations at Ostia.
The entrance to the Museums and Galleries is on Viale Vaticano.
The Pigna (Pine-cone) Courtyard is found near the entrance to the museums, and it was designed by Bramante when he united the Palazzetto of

Detail of the *Sarcaphagus of Costantina* (Museum Pio-Clementino).

Left: room at the Vatican Museum.

Entrance to the Vatican Museum.

63

Innocent VIII to the Palazzo Pontificio. It takes its name from a monumental bronze pine-cone that rests on a capital in front of the apse; it is the work of Bramante. In the center of the courtyard there is a statue of St. Peter, built as a memorial of the First Vatican Council.

The Pio Clementino Museum

Founded by Clement XIV and Pius VI the museum is located in the rooms of the Palazzetto of Innocent VIII and in those constructed by Simonetti on the orders of Pius VI: the *Sala a Croce Greca*, the *Sala Rotonda*, the *Sala delle Muse*, the *Sala degli Animali*, and it includes a part of the *Galleria delle Statue*.

Sala a Croce Greca: This room was designed by Simonetti in neo-classical style. At the two sides of the entrance there are granite sphinxes. Worthy of note are the sarcophagus of porphyry of *Constance*, daughter of Constantine the Emperor in the IV century, and the sarcophagus of St. Helena, the mother of the emperor. *A shield with the bust of Minerva and the phases of the moon* (III century) is in the middle of the room.

Sala Rotonda: This room was designed by Simonetti, who took his inspiration from the Pantheon. The walls are full of niches divided by high pilasters. Ancient mosaics adorn the floors. In the center there is a huge porphyry basin which came from the Domus Aurea. In the niches there are statues

Pio Clementino Museum.
Above: Sala Rotonda.
Below: Sala Croce Greca.

Egyptian Museum.
a room in the
Above: detail of

of divinities and semi-divine heroes. Busts, statues, and portraits complete the room.

Sala delle Muse: This room takes its name from the statues of the *Muses* that are displayed here. Some of these statues, found near Tivoli, are reproductions of ancient Greek sculptures. Sebastiano Conca decorated the ceiling with frescoes representing *Apollo* and the *Muses*. In the vestibule behind the room there is an antique relief with scenes of *Pyrrhic dancing*.

Sala degli Animali: Pius VI entrusted the realization of this room to the architect Francesco Franzoni. There are gathered here figures of animals of previous workmanship, among which a green porphyry crab and various groups, such as *The Sacrifice of Mithras*, and *Meleager with the dog and the head of the wild boar that was killed*. The floor is in mosaic and comes in part from Palestrina. On the walls there are two small mosaics representing bulls being attacked by lions.

GALLERIA DELLE STATUE: This is situated in the *Palazzetto del Belvedere del Pollaiolo* and was decorated by Mantegna and students of Pinturicchio. The most important work here is the *Apollo Sauroctono*, a copy of the bronze by Praxiteles. Also worthy of note are the statue of *Hermes*, the *Eros of Centocelle* (copy of a Greek original of the IV century), *The Wounded Amazon*, and the *Sleeping Ariadne* (Hellenistic art of the III-II century B.C.). Numerous other works, among which two candelbra of the II century and a beautiful alabaster tub, complete the gallery.

GALLERIA DEI BUSTI: In four rooms divided by columns we find the busts of the Roman emperors, among which (in the first room) those of *Caracalla, Octavian as a Youth*, and *Julius Caesar*. Among the other works on display there is the famous statue of *Jupiter Enthroned* in the third room.

GABINETTO DELLE MASCHERE: This room owes its name to the mosaic floor which represents some masks. The ceiling by Domenico De Angelis was inspired by mythology. Among the statues are the *Venus of Cnidus*, a copy of the original by Praxiteles of the IV century B.C., and the *Three Graces*, another Roman copy of a Greek original.

Passing again through the Sala degli Animali, we enter the *Cortile del Belvedere*, designed by Bramante, built by Giacomo di Pietrasanta, and transformed by Simonetti with the addition of a portal in Yonic style with pavilions. The pavilions in the four corners are called « gabinetti » and take their names from the works that are in them. The most important is the « gabinetto » of *Laocoòn*, which shows Laocoon and his sons in the serpent's coils. The monument, an original of the Hellenistic period of the first century B.C. was rediscovered in 1506 among the ruins of the temple of Titus on the Esquiline Hill.

This is followed by the « Gabinetto » of the *Apollo Belvedere*, containing the refined and perfect statue reproduced from an original in bronze of the IV century B.C. by Leochares. Then there is the « Gabinetto » of the *Perseus*, with the work by Canova (1800) placed between the two wrestlers Creugante

Above:
Sacramentario Gelasiano, tempera on parchment.

Below:
Diptych of Rambona,
ivory bas-relief.

and Damosseno, also by Canova. Then comes the « Gabinetto » of the *Hermes* with the statue of the god, falsely believed to be a portrait of Antinoos, and which is a copy of an original of the school of Praxiteles found near Castel Sant'Angelo.

Crossing the courtyard we enter the *Vestibolo Rotondo* where we find the statue of the *Apoxyòmenos*, a copy of an original bronze by Lisippo (ca. 330 B.C.).

To the right of the *Vestibolo Rotondo* is the *Atrio del Torso del Belvedere*. Of the original statue of *Hercules* sitting on a wild boar's skin, there remains only the torso. The sculpture, perfect in its lines and admired by Michelangelo, is the work of the Athenian Apollonio (I century B.C.). In the same room we find the *Ara Casalis*, presumed to be a cippus of a statue and adorned with reliefs (III-II century).

The Chiaramonti Museum

The museum takes its name from the family of Pope Pius VII (1800-1823) and is divided into three sections: the *Galleria Chiaramonti*, the *Galleria Lapidaria*, and the *Braccio Nuovo*.

Bramante designed the long corridor that joins the Palazzetto of Innocent VIII with the Palazzo Pontificio. The *Galleria Chiaramonti* makes up part of this corridor. Divided into sixty sections, it brings together numerous sculptures, from Greek originals to copies of statues of gods, portraits, urns, sarcophagi, altars, and various fragments. Among the most interesting pieces are a Roman sarcophagus of the

Detail of the *Rotulo* of Joshua, tempera on parchment.

Detail of a piece of Byzantine cloth representing the Annunciation.

II century A.D. with scenes from the myth of *Alcestes*; the statues of *Hercules* and *Telephorus*, the statue of *Igea*, copies of Greek originals of the IV century B.C., and *Ganimede and the Eagle* (a copy of an original bronze of Leochares of the IV century B.C.).

GALLERIA LAPIDARIA: This is situated in the remaining part of Bramante's corridor, and it contains more than 5,000 pagan and Christian inscriptions, some coming from the catacombs. The *Braccio Nuovo* of the gallery was constructed between 1817 and 1822 by order of Pius VII, and it is so named to distinguish it from the one designed by Fontana and intended to be a library. In the great room with the barrel vaulting and the niches containing statues we note precious mosaics on the floor at the sides. These are from a villa of the II century situated on Via Ardeatina. In this room, too, there are valuable works. The *Nile* of the Hellenic period is here. (The river, lying near a sphinx, has in his hand a cornucopia full of fruits and flowers, symbols of fertility, and on his body there are 16 putti). There are also the *Resting Satyr*, a copy of Praxiteles, the statue of *Augustus* found at Prima Porta, the *Doriforo* and the *Wounded Amazon*, both copies of Policletus; and *Demosthenes* of 280 B.C

The Vatican Library

From the very beginning of the Christian era, the popes collected documents and later incunabula and books. Nicholas V (1447-1455) founded the first real library, which was enriched by Sixtus IV, who also had it decorated and furnished by Melozzo da Forlì and by the Ghirlandaio brothers. Sixtus V (1585-1590) made it still larger, entrusting the work to Domenico Fontana, who constructed the room which became known as the *Salone Sistino*. Together with the *Galleria Clementina*, the *Sala Alessandrina*, the *Sale Paoline*, the *Sale Sistine*, and the *Galleria di Urbano III*, the *Salone Sistino* constitutes the seat of the Vatican Library. The *Salone Sistino* is divided into two naves by pilasters with frescoes representing the inventors of the alphabet. On the walls there are more frescoes showing ancient Rome and episodes from the life of Sixtus V. Rare and precious manuscripts are displayed in the showcases. Among these there are the *Codice Vaticano B* of the Bible (IV century), the *Virgili* (*Virgilio Vaticano* of the IV century, *Virgilio Palatino* and *Virgilio Romano* of the V century), the famous codice palinsesto with the *De Republica* of Cicero (I century), the *Breviario* of Mattia Corvino (1487) and the original manuscript of the *Canzoniere* by Petrarch.

The Library in its entirety is composed of about 700,000 printed volumes, 60,000 codices, and 7,000 incunabula.

In the *Galleria di Urbano III* there is a collection of XVI century astronomical instruments.

MUSEO SACRO DELLA BIBLIOTECA (Sacred Museum of the Library)

The museum, founded by Benedict XIV, offers a collection of the minor Christian arts. Here we find objects, in bronze, gold, enamel, ivory, and ceramic, in addition to papyri found in

Detail of the
Martyrdom of St. Elmione,
tempera on parchment.

Detail of a Byzantine
miniature of
Noah's Ark.

the catacombs. In the last two rooms the treasure of the *Sancta Sanctorum*, sumptuous in its Byzantine enamels and jewels, is kept.

The Sala delle Nozze Aldobrandini: This room takes its name from the Roman fresco of the first century—one of the best preserved masterpieces of the Augustan age—found on the Esquiline Hill in 1605. The vault of the room has frescoes by Guido Reni.

MUSEO PROFANO DELLA BIBLIO-TECA (The Secular Museum of the Library)

This is composed of only one room that contains objects from many different places. Here are preserved sculptures, statues, and ivory objects of the Etruscan and Roman periods. Begun under Clement XIII in 1767, it was completed by Pius VI (1775-1799). On the ceiling there is a manificent fresco of *Minerva e il Tempo*.

Worthy of note is the head of *Augustus* and that of *Nero*, both in bronze, and a Roman mosaic of the second century, coming from Hadrian's Villa.

APPARTAMENTO BORGIA (The Borgia Apartment)

Alexander VI, the Borgia pope, lived here until his death. The apartment is composed of six rooms, four of which belong to the old edifice of Nicholas V. The other two rooms were built by order of Alexander VI in a square tower called the *Borgia Tower*.

Sala delle Sibille (*Room of the Sibyls*): In the twelve lunettes of the double vault there are the figures of the *Sibyls* and the *Prophets*, the work of students of Pinturicchio.

Sala del Credo (*Room of the Creed*): The frescoes of Pier Mattia d'Amelia represent the *Twelve Apostles* coupled with the same number of *Prophets* in order to demonstrate the continuity from the *Old Testament* to the *New Testament*. The room takes its name from the bands with verses from the *Credo* that each Apostle has in his hand.

Sala delle Scienze e delle Arti Liberali (*Room of the Sciences and of the Liberal Arts*): Antonio da Viterbo, also

Above: detail of the *Disputa di S. Caterina d'Alessandria* by Pinturicchio.

Left: *Disputa di S. Caterina d'Alessandria* commissioned by Pope Alexander VI for the Sala dei Santi in the Borgia Apartment.

On the right: Room in the Borgia Apartment.

Above: *Madonna with Child*
by Vitale da Bologna
(Vatican Pinacoteca).

Left: detail of
The Last Judgment
by Giovanni e Niccolò
(Vatican Pinacoteca).

Right: a Byzantine miniature
representing *David
Between the Personifications
of Wisdom and Prophecy*
(Sacred Museum).

called Pastura, has represented the symbols of the arts and sciences in the frescoes in the lunettes.

Sala dei Santi (Room of the Saints): This is the work of Pinturicchio. The marvelous frescoes represent scenes from the *Old and New Testaments*: the *Dispute of St. Catherine of Alexandria with the Philosophers in the Presence of the Emperor Massimiano, St. Paul the Hermit, St. Anthony,* the *Martyrdom of St. Sebastian.* On the ceiling there are the myths of *Iris, Osiride, Io,* and the *Bull Api.* Above the door there is the *Madonna and Child* by Pinturicchio also.

Sala dei Misteri della Fede (Room of the Mysteries of the Faith): The frescoes by Pinturicchio represent the seven mysteries in the lives of Jesus and Mary (the *Annunciation,* the *Nativity,* the *Epiphany,* the *Resurrection,* the *Ascension, Pentecost,* and the *Assumption of the Virgin*). In the fresco of the *Resurrection,* at the bottom left, Pinturicchio has drawn Pope Alexander VI in pontifical robes.

Sala dei Pontefici (Room of the Pontiffs): The room has the vault decorated with plaster figures and frescoes by Perin del Vaga and Giovanni da Udine (XVI century); they represent allegories and the signs of the zodiac. On the walls there are six tapestries of the Flemish school (XVI century).

Sistine Chapel

Its construction, by order of Sixtus IV, was begun by Giovannino de' Dolci in 1473. Designed to be a private chapel for the popes and also for the most solemn ceremonies of the Holy See, it

Perspective view of the interior

of the magnificent
Sistine Chapel.

is also the site of the Conclaves which elect the new pope. The chapel measures 40.50 meters in length, 13.10 meters in width, and 20.70 meters in height. It is divided into two parts by a marble balustrade by Mino da Fiesole and Andrea Bregno, who were also the designers of the *Choir* on the right side. Michelangelo, with the marvellous frescoes on the ceiling and the back wall, together with other artists who collaborated, has left us one of the most important monuments of the Renaissance. On the wide sides there are the *Choir* and the *Papal Throne.*

On the side walls there are twelve frescoes, the works of various artists of the XV century, representing on the left side *Events from the life of Moses* and on the right *Events in the Life of Jesus Christ.* The scenes from Moses' life are the *Trip to Egypt* by Perugino, the *Calling* by Sandro Botticelli, the *Crossing of the Red Sea* and *Moses Receiving the Tables of the Law* by Cosimo Rosselli, the *Punishment of the Sons of Core* by Botticelli, and the *Testament* and the *Death of Moses* by Luca Signorelli.

The scenes from the life of Christ are the *Baptism of Christ* by Pinturicchio, the *Temptation of Jesus* and the *Healing of the Leper* by Botticelli, the *Calling of the Apostles* by Ghirlandaio, the *Sermon on the Mount* by Rosselli, the *Giving of the Keys* by Perugino, and the *Last Supper* by Rosselli.

On the wall opposite the altar there are two frescoes redone by A. Fiammingo and Matteo da Lecce in the XVI century (Originally they were by Ghirlandaio and Salviati). Between the windows, in the niches, there are portraits of popes by Ghirlandaio, Botticelli, Rosselli, and other painters.

But the greatest frescoes of the Sistine Chapel are without a doubt those by Michelangelo who was given the task by Pope Julius II, the nephew of Sixtus IV and who dedicated long and toilsome years of work to it. Michelangelo's work covers the great spaces on the ceiling, the back wall and in part the upper parts of the side walls. Biblical scenes are represented on the ceiling: *God divides the light from the darkness*, *God creates the Sun, the Moon and the Stars*, *God separates the Land from the Waters*, the *Creation of Man* (One of the most suggestive scenes is the one in which the Creator leans over the splendid figure of the inert Adam to give him life), the *Creation of Woman*, the *Expulsion from Paradise*, the *Sacrifice of Noah*, the *Great Flood*, and the *Drunkenness of Noah*. On the side walls there are, alternating with each other, gigantic figures of the *Prophets* and the *Sibyls* and the *Ancestors* of Christ. In the lunettes above the windows there are the *Torture of Aman* the *Bronze Serpent, Judith Cutting of the Head of Holofernes*, and the *Slaying of Goliath*.

The fresco of the *Last Judgment* (that covers a wall of 200 square meters) was painted by Michelangelo when he was already over 60 years old. To complete it, two windows were walled up and previous frescoes by Perugino and by Michelangelo himself were destroyed. In the upper part, at the center the great figure of Christ stands out, in the dazzling attitude of the Judge. To his right the elect float up to heaven; to his left the throng of the damned whirl in tumult, thrown down below where, with

Above: The Creation of Man.

Below: The Last Judgment.

the boat ready, the inexorable Charon waits. In the right corner there is a divinity of the infernal regions, Minos, to whom the artist, according to Vasari, gave the features of Biagio da Cesena, the papal master of ceremonies who continually criticized Michelangelo harshly. In the lower part at the left is the *Resurrection of the Dead.* In the center there is a group of angels intent on blowing their trumpets. Around Christ there are the Madonna, St. John the Baptist, St. Andrew with his special cross, St. Peter with the keys, and St. Paul. At the feet of Christ we see St. Laurence with the grill, and St. Bartholomew, who holds in his hand his own skin torn from his body (On the skin Michelangelo has left his own self portrait like a sort of dark watermark). To the left of this group there are the Holy Women. At the right we notice, among the other figures, Simon of Cyrene with the cross of Christ, the good thief Dismas with his own cross, St. Sebastian, and St. Catherine with the Wheel.

Atmospheric conditions, the smoke from candles, some careless restorations, and the drapings painted in by Daniele da Volterra (who thus earned himself the nickname of « braghettone » = « pants putter on ») to cover up the most critical parts of the sacred nudes (the figures were originally completely nude) have changed in part the chromatic equilibrium of the composition.

Rooms of Raphael

These are situated above the Borgia Apartment and were begun by Nicholas II. Towards the end of 1508 Julius

Detail of the
Dispute of the Sacrament.

Detail of the *School of Athens* by Raphael.

II gave Raphael, who was only 25 years old, the task of decorating his apartment with frescoes. Raphael worked there from 1508 until his death, and the work was finished by his students. The four rooms were decorated in chronological order (*Segnatura, Eliodoro, Incendio, and Costantino.* However, the topographical order is different, beginning with that of the Incendio, followed by those of the Segnatura, Eliodoro, and Costantino.

The *Sala dell'Incendio* (the *Room of the Fire*) was the last painted by Raphael. It was inspired by the *Burning of Borgo* and refers to the episode in which Leo IV (847-855) is said to have extinguished the fire in Borgo Santo Spirito by making the sign of the cross. The scene recalls the description by Virgil of the burning of Troy. In the fresco we note in the background the flames that threaten the Basilica of St. Peter and toward the right the pope standing at a window of the Vatican Palace and giving his blessing. In the foreground the people beg for help and try to put out the flames. And finally, at the left there is the burning of Troy with Aeneas escaping and carrying his father on his shoulders. He is followed by his son and his wife.

The *Giustificazione di Leone III* (*Justification of Leo III*) represents the episode in which the pontiff justifies himself in answer to the calumnies of his adversaries in the medieval Basilica of St. Peter. The work is attributed by some to Giulio Romano, by others to Perin del Vaga. The *Coronation of Charlemagne* is also attributed to Giulio Romano while the fresco of the *Naval Victory of Leo IV Over the Saracens* was executed for the most part by the same painter. On the ceiling of the room the decoration of Perugino is conserved. He painted the glorification of the Holy Trinity in four round sections. Raphael and his students painted the rest of the ceiling with subjects referring to the lives of Leo III and Leo IV but with the purpose of exalting the pontificate of Leo X. The *Stanza della Segnatura* (*Room of the Tribunal of the Holy See*): This room is called thus because it was destined to be the Ecclesiastical Tribunal of the Holy See. It was the first to be decorated by Raphael. On the ceiling in four medallions *Theology*, *Justice*, *Philosophy*, and *Poetry* are symbolically represented. In correspondence with the four corners of the ceiling and alternating with the medallions, the *Judgment of Solomon*, *Astronomy*, *Apollo and Marsyas*, the *Dispute of the Holy Sacrament*, and the *Glorification of the Eucharist* are painted. This last composition is divided into two parts. In the upper part the *Glory of Heaven* is represented. In the lower part there is an assembly of the representatives of the Church who took part in the dispute about the sacrament of the Eucharist.

The *Scuola di Atene* (*School of Athens*) represents the triumph of Philosophy and depicts a huge room with two colossal statues of Minerva and Apollo. Here are painted the greatest philosophers and wise men of antiquity and some artists and princes of the Renaissance. These personages make a circle around Plato and Aristotle who advance from the back of the room talking with each other.

The frescoes on the skirting board are the *Siege of Syracuse*, the *Death of*

Detail of the *Incendio di Borgo.*

Messa di Bolsena, detail.

Archimedes, Wise Men Discussing the Celestial Sphere and *Philosophy* by Perin del Vaga.

The *Stanza di Eliodoro* (the *Room of Heliodorus*): The theme of the frescoes is the miraculous intervention of God in order to protect the Church. On the entrance wall there is *Leo I that Stops the Invasion of Attila*, on the right wall the *Miracle of Bolsena*. (In 1263, the consecrated Host bled during the Mass, spotting the corporal of a doubtful priest); the miracle inspired the Bull with which Urban IV instituted the feast of Corpus Christi in 1264. The fresco on the left wall depicts the *Driving of Heliodorus from the Temple*. Heliodorus, treasurer of the king of Syria, Seleuco Filopatore, on orders from his lord, went to Jerusalem to sack the Temple. When he was about to complete the sacrilegious robbery, there appeared a knight and two young men sent by God and armed with twigs. They stopped Heliodorus and put his men to flight. In the background of the fresco we see the figure of Pope Jullius II.

On the last wall there is the fresco of the *Liberation of St. Peter*. The Apostle is led out of the prison by an angel that passes through the sleeping guards. This is a work with special effects of light.

Sala di Costantino (Room of Constantine): This was painted by Raphael's students after the death of the master. The room takes its name from the great frescoes that depict the most important deeds of the emperor: the *Baptism of Constantine* by Francesco Penni, the *Donation of Constantine* by Raffaele del Colle, the *Apparition of the Cross*

Above: Freeing of St. Peter from prison.

Below: Pope Leo I stops Attila and the Huns.

to Constantine by Giulio Romano. Also by Giulio Romano is the large fresco of the *Battle of Constantine* that alludes to the emperor's victory over Maxentius at the Milvian Bridge. In this composition, full of life and movement, we see Constantine at the center, advancing on his white horse and carrying the cross and the standard, while two angels point out Massentius, who is drowning in the river. On the ceiling the *Triumph of Christianity* by Tommaso Laureti is painted. On the skirting board there are other scenes from the life of Constantine.

LOGGE DI RAFFAELLO

This large gallery overlooking the courtyard of San Damaso is composed of 13 arcades, whose vaults are decorated with scenes from the Old and New Testaments. The subjects of the fres-

Egyptian Museum: anfora depicting Achilles and Ajax playing dice. (530 B.C.).

Capitoline Museums: *Saint Sebastian* by Guido Reni.

coes, painted by Raphael, Giulio Romano, Perin del Vaga and Penni: *The Creation*, the stories of *Adam and Eve, Noah, Abraham, Isaac, Jacob, Joseph, Joshua, David, Solomon* and *Jesus*.

GALLERIA DELLE CARTE GEOGRAFICHE (Hall of the maps)
The long gallery (approximately 360 feet) takes its name from the 40 maps of Italy which decorate its walls. The maps were painted by Ignazio Danti of Perugia, a famous cartographer, mathematician and architect, between 1580 and 1583.

GALLERIA DEGLI ARAZZI (Hall of the tapestries)
This very long corridor contains a collection of the largest and most valuable tapestries in existence. They are mostly Flemish, but some are Italian. The most important of the latter depict events during the pontificate of Urban VIII.

GALLERIA DEI CANDELABRI (Gallery of the candelabras)
So named because of the marble candelabras (originally in the Roman churches of Santa Costanza and Sant'Agnese), the hall also has a collection of antique sarcophagi and statues. The vault was decorated by Torti and Ludwig Seitz with episodes from the pontificate of Leo XIII.

SALA DELLA BIGA (Hall of the chariot)
The Hall was commissioned by Pope Pius VI and constructed after a design by Camporese. In the center of the round, cupolaed room is a *biga*, or chariot, the work of Franzoni (1788)

82

Incorporated in the sculpture are fragmets of marbles from as early as the first century A.D., as well as more modern ones. Part of the horse on the right is antique, as is the seat of the chariot (first century A.D.). The latter was formerly used as the bishop's chair in the Roman church of San Marco.

CAPPELLA DI NICCOLÒ V (Chapel of Niccolò V)

Known also as the Beato Angelico Chapel, the room is dedicated to Sts. Lawrence and Stephen. It was painted in the 15th century by Fra' Giovanni da Fiesole, better known as Fra' Angelico, for Pope Niccolò V.
Scenes from the life of St. Stephan alternate with portraits (on the pilasters) of doctors of the Church. The four Evangelists are pictured in the cupola. Signs of the zodiac and the sun are worked in the marble pavement.

SALA DELLA IMMACOLATA (Hall of the Immaculate Conception)

This room, frescoed by Podesti (1800-1895), recalls the solemn definition of the dogma of the Immaculate Conception, proclaimed by Pius IX on December 8, 1854. On the walls are the Sibyls who, according to tradition, prophesied the divine motherhood of Mary. The medallions of the vault present episodes from the lives of Esther and Judith, as well as the allegorical figures of Faith and Theology.

MUSEO EGIZIO (The Egyptian museum)

The museum was established in 1839 by Pope Gregory XVI. There are ten rooms with items from other museums

A view of the Chapel of Nicholas V.

Capitoline Museums: *Baptism of Christ* by Titian.

and from Hadrian's villa at Tivoli. There are also many items which were received as gifts from Egypt.

Room I (Room of the Sarcophagi) has, among others, three black basalt sarcophagi from the 6th century B.C. The room also contains statues of deities with animal heads.

Room II (Room of the Statues) has a remarkable head of the Pharaoh Mentuhotep, dated 2000 B.C.

Room III (Room of the Imitations) contains works by Roman artists of the second and third centuries A.D. which make use of Egyptian motifs. The best-known of these are a statue of the Nile and a bust of Isis.

Room IV (Room of the *naophorus*) contarins a basalt statuette of a *naophorus*, a priest carrying a small temple, from the 6th century B.C.

Room V (Hemicycle Room), so-called because it follows the curve of the Cortile della Pigna (Pinecone Courtyard). The room has an exhibit of sarcophagy and mummies.

Above: anfora showing the departure of the *Dioscuri* Egyptian Museum.

MUSEO ETRUSCO (Etruscan museum)

Founded by Pope Gregory XVI, the museum has a valuable collection of objects excavated over the years in southern Etruria. Among the items are sarcophagi, bronzes, cinerary urns, statues, vases and amphoras from the archaic period, as well as Attic, Italiot and Etruscan vases. Of great interest in the second room of the museum is the Regolini-Galassi tomb (650 B.C.), brought from Cerveteri in 1873. The third room has the *Mars of Todi*, and in the twelfth room is found a stele from Palestrina dating from the 5th century B.C.

Below: *Pegasus*, Museo Gregoriano Etrusco.

PINACOTECA VATICANA (The Vatican Gallery of Paintings)

The gallery, in Lombard Renaissance style, was done by Luca Beltramini on commission from Pope Pius XI. It contains the collections from an earlier gallery, founded by Pius VI in 1797, as well as a collection of contemporary works added by Pius XII.

The collection is composed of paintings from the Byzantine period up to the present. Among them are the large altar-frontal of the *Universal Judgment* (11th-12th centuries); the *Madonna and Child with Saints*, by Giovanni Bonsi (14th century); a *Christ Blessing* of the Byzantine school; *St. Francis*, by Margaritone d'Arezzo (12th century); the Stefaneschi *Polyptych*, by Giotto; consisting of *Christ Enthroned Surrounded by Angels, The Martyrdoms of Peter and Paul, Peter Enthroned with the Apostles James and Paul, the Evangelists Mark and John on Either Side of the Throne*; the *Madonna of the Magnificat*, by Bernardino Daddi (14th century); *Christ Blessing*, by Simone Martini (1285-1344); *Scenes from the Life of San Nicola da Bari* and *Virgin and Child with Sts. Dominic and Catherine*, by Fra' Angelico; *The Coronation of the Virgin*, by Fra' Filippo Lippi (1406-1469); the 14 fragments of the fresco *The Ascension of Christ*, which was originally in the apse of the Roman Church of the Holy Apostles; the *Angelic Musicians*, also by Melozzo da Forlì and from the same basilica; and the large fresco by Melozzo, *Sixtus IV Appointing Bartolomeo Secchi, Called Il Platina, as Vatican Librarian*.

Of equal interest are a *Madonna Enthroned*, by Perugino (1445-1523), *The*

85

Leonardo da Vinci:
St. Jerome.

Giotto and students:
Detail of the Stefaneschi
Polyptych.

Coronation of the Virgin and *The Madonna with Christ Child Belessing*, by Pinturicchio.

Raphael is also represented, with *The Coronation of the Virgin, The Madonna of Foligno,* and *The Transfiguration.* In the section devoted to Leonardo da Vinci (1452-1519) are found an unfinished *St. Jerome* and *The Burial of Christ,* called the *Pietà,* by Giovanni Bellini.

Among the masterpieces of the Venetian school are the *Madonna di San Nicolò dei Frari,* by Titian (1477-1576); *St. Helen,* by Veronese (1528-1588); *St. Bernard,* by Sebastiano dal Piombo (1485-1547); and other works from the late Renaissance and early Baroque. Continuing through the rooms we find works by Flemish, French, Italian, Dutch and German artists, among which are the *St. Francis Xavier* by Van Dyke (1599-1641) and *Fortune,* by Guido Reni.

The contemporary collection contains works by Utrillo, Sironi, De Chirico, Carrà, Morandi, Rosai, De Pisis, Rodin and Messina.

MUSEO PROFANO (Museum of Pagan Art) .

Founded by Gregory XVI in the Lateran Palace, the museum was transferred by John XXIII to the Vatican. The collection is made up of antique sculpture, mainly copies of Greek originals from the Classical period, but there are also some Roman originals which date from the end of the Republican era to the Imperial era. Among the pieces are funeral altars and sarcophagi decorated with mosaics, from Caracalla's baths. There is also a remarkable collection of epitaphs.

Melozzo da Forlì:
*Inauguration of the
Vatican Library.*

Caravaggio: *Deposition
of Christ.*

MUSEO CRISTIANO (The Christian Museum)

The museum was founded by Pius IX in 1854. Of great interest are the fragments of sarcophagi figuring the *Birth of the Messiah* and the *Epiphany.* Among the most important works are a sarcophagus from the 4th century A.D., a sarcophagus with the *Red Sea Passage*, a statue of the *Good Shepherd*, largely restored, and, of particular interest, the front of a sarcophagus which was originally in the Basilica of St. Lawrence Outside the Walls. This bas-relief shows a youthful Jesus with the twelve Apostles. In the foreground are twelve sheep, symbolically representing Jesus' flock.

MUSEO MISSIONARIO ETNOLOGICO (The Ethnological Missionary Museum)

Created by Pius XI in 1926, the museum was first located in the Lateran Palace. It was transferred to the Vatican by John XXIII.

Originally it comprised 40,000 items from the missionary exhibition held during Holy Year 1925, which were offered to the Pope by vicarates, apostolic prefectures, missions, archdioceses, dioceses, missionary orders and institutes, religious communities, private persons and institutes from all over the world. To this nucleus were added other collections and individual items, the first of which, by the order of the Pope, came from the store-rooms of the Vatican Museum. The Congregation of Propagation of the Faith offered what remained of the Borgia Museum collections. Examples of Indian art were acquired and over the years gifts came from every country in the world.

Basilica of St. John Lateran

The basilica of St. John Lateran « *Omnium Urbis et Orbis ecclesiarum Mater et Caput* », as it was defined by Clement XII, is the cathedral of Rome and Mother Church of Christianity. Even after the popes had abandoned the Lateran and had left Rome for Avignon, later returning and establishing themselves in the Vatican, the *Basilica Lateranense* remained the episcopal church of Peter's successors. The basilica is thus the supreme expression of both a local Roman church and the

Above: Basilica of San Giovanni in Laterano, cathedral of the bishop of Rome.

Left: detail of the baldichin where the relics of the Princes of the Apostles are kept.

Below: the central nave.

universal church, united in the person of the Pope. From it the Pope exercises, symbolically, his function as pastor not only of Rome but of the entire world. Here he humbly presides over the Communion of the Bishops, who are, like him, successors to the Apostles. St. John Lateran is one of the four Roman basilicas having a Porta Santa (Holy Gate). In 313 A.D. the Emperor Constantine gave the houses of the Plauzi Laterani family to Pope Melchiades, and along with them, the nearby military barracks of the *Equites Singulares*, expressing the desire that a church should be built on the site, as well as a palace for the Bishops of Rome, that is, the Popes.

The early basilica was dedicated to the Holy Savior and had five naves supported by columns. The façade was adorned with a mosaic portrait of the Savior surrounded by angels in adoration. This was the first image from the Christian rites to appear outside the catacombs. The basilica has been frequently damaged: Leo I had it restored in the 5th century after it had been devastated by Genseric's Vandals; in the 8th century Pope Hadrian ordered another restoration. Destroyed by the earthquake of 896 it was reconstructed by Pope Sergius III in the 10th century and dedicated to Sts. John the Baptist and John the Evangelist. Later popes have added to its richness and beauty.

In 1300 Boniface VIII proclaimed the first Jubilee Year from St. John Lateran. With the transfer of the papacy to Avignon the Basilica was abandoned. In 1308 it was destroyed by fire. Rebuilt, it was again destroyed by fire in 1360.

Pope Leo XIII's
sepulcher by Tadolini.

The splendid mosaic
of the apse.

Urban V had it completely rebuilt by
the Sienese architect Giovanni di Stefano. Martin V, Eugene IV, and other
popes continued with the work of restoration and enrichment. In the 17th
century Innocent X put Francesco Borromini in charge of its reconstruction
for the Holy Year 1650.

The principal façade (eastern) is ap-
proached from the Piazza San Giovanni
in Laterano. The façade is the work
of the Florentine architect Alessandro
Galilei, on commission from Clement
XII.

Simple and majestic, it is of two stories,
each having a loggia with five entrances.
A third loggia is crowned by a statue
of the Savior and 14 statues of saints
and apostles. On the left, in the
portico, is a statue of Constantine
which was found in his baths. Coupled
columns and pilasters rest on a tall
basement upon which appears the coat
of arms of Clement XII; they support
the fronton, which is surmounted by a
tympanum in which two angels hold
an ancient image of the Savior.

The portico has five doors, each with a
loggia above it (the central one is reserved for the benediction of the popes).
The center door is of bronze and is
believed to have come from the *curia
ostilia.* The farthest door to the right
is the Porta Santa.

The interior of the basilica is grandiose
and solemn, with five naves and a
transept. It is about 390 feet long, in
the form of a Latin cross. The church
is baroque and looks much the same
as it did when Borromini designed it
for Innocent X. In the central nave
between the columns and pilasters, are
niches with enormous baroque statues
of the Apostles, by pupils of Bernini.

The stucco bas-reliefs above, designed by Algardi, present scenes from the Old Testament (on the left) and the New Testament (on the right). Higher up are the large oval portraits of the prophets. The rich ceiling (6th century) is decorated with symbols of the Church and the Passion and the coats of arms of three popes: Pius IV, Pius V, and Pius VI. The crests are enclosed by ornamental frames designed by Daniele da Volterra. The cosmatesque pavement is from the 15th century, done by the orders of Martin V.

In the center of the transept is a Gothic tabernacle by Giovanni De Stefano, on orders from Urban V. The frescoes are by Barna da Siena. The heads of Sts. Peter and Paul, in silver wrappings, are preserved in this tabernacle. Beneath the tabernacle is the Papal Altar, the only altar in the world which is not of *Pietra Santa* but of a piece of wood which legend says was that used by St. Peter when he officiated at the Mass. In the Confession is the tomb of Martin V.

Toward the end of the 16th century the transept was redone and its walls decorated with frescoes. In the right arm is the great organ, upheld by two columns, and toward the presbytery is found the tomb of Innocent III (by G. Lucchetti, 1891). At the back of the presbytery is the rich Altar of the Sacrament.

The apse, reconstructed in 1884 along with the baptistery by order of Leo XIII, is the work of Virginio and Francesco Vespignani. In the semidome, whose restored mosaic was formerly in the old apse, is the figure of Christ surrounded by angels and clouds. Below, the Dove of the Holy Spirit, with

Monument to St. Francis and facade of the Basilica.

General view of the Cloister.

streaming rays symbolizing the Holy Trinity and illuminating a cross at the center of which is figured the Baptism of Christ. The cross rises at the top of a hill, on which a symbolic Jerusalem is located, represented as a fortress guarded by an angel. At the center of the hill is the Tree of Life and next to it the phoenix, symbol of the Resurrection. Four rivers, from which sheep are drinking, descend the hill and become united as the Jordan. They are symbolic of the four Evangelists.

At the sides of the cross are, on the left, the Virgin, St. Peter and St. Paul. On the right are St. John the Baptist, St. John the Evangelist and St. Andrew. Kneeling in front of the Virgin is the donor of the work, Pope Nicolò IV, a Franciscan. By his wish, St. Francis (between the Virgin and St. Peter) and St. Anthony of Padua (between the two Sts. John) also appear in the work. On the lower edge, in the space between the windows, are the Apostles. A marble bishop's chair of recent date, decorated with small twisted columns is in the back of the apse.

The wall over the Altar of the Sacrament has a fresco of *The Ascension of Our Lord*, by the Cavalier d'Arpino (1550-1640).

In the tympanum is figured the Eternal Father Blessing, a work by Pomarancio. On the altar, designed by Pietro Paolo Olivieri (1551-1599) and commissioned by Clement VIII, is a jeweled ciborium in the shape of a small temple. Above, in gilded bronze, is the Last Supper, supported by two bronze angels. Behind the altar is a very old table, which legend says was that of the Last Supper. Around the

The basilica of St. John seen from the Walls.

Right: detail of the ceiling.

The Palazzo del Laterano, up to 1000 residence of the Popes, today seat of the Cardinal Vicar of Rome.

altar are marble statues of Elias, Moses, Melchisedec and Aaron.

The Roman vault was restored by Clement VIII, who also, in 1593, ordered the construction of a large organ to cover the entire wall above the side door. The walls of the Roman vault have colored and gilded frescoes (from design by Giacomo Della Porta) with the history of the basilica and the conversion of Constantine. One of the best of these is the *Baptism of Constantine*, by Pomarancio (1562).

The choir, to the right of the altar, is by Girolamo Rainaldi (1570-1655) and was commissioned by Filippo Colonna. The wooden choirstalls are from the 16th century and decorated with small columns and statues. The vault has a gilded stucco decoration; in its center is a fresco by Baldasserino (1558-1628) of the *Coronation of the Virgin*. On the altar, surrounded by decorations in metal and colored marble, is the painting *Christ with St. John the Baptist and St. John the Evangelist*. At the other side of the Roman vault, in the Chapel of the Crucifix, is a marble fragment which is believed to be part of a monument to Nicolò IV, attributed to Adeodato di Cosma (13th century).

Over the altar in the St. John the Evangelist Chapel is a fresco of the saint by Lorenzo Galdi (1624-1703). Also of interest are the cosmatesque tomb of Cardinal Casati di Giussano. the tomb of Pope Sergius IV (1012) and the imposing monument to Alexander VIII. The simple and spacious Massimo Chapel is the work of Giacomo Della Porta.

The Torlonia Chapel, in marble and gold, enclosed by a beautiful bronze gate, was built by Raimondi in the first half of the last century. Over the altar, decorated in malachite and lapis-lazuli, is a *Deposition*, by Tenerani. The beautiful rosettes of the ceiling are reproduced in the pavement. In the four corners of the chapel are statues representing the four virtues: Prudence, Justice, Strength and Temperance. Above them are portraits of the Evangelists.

Proceeding, we see a fragment of a fresco of Boniface VIII surrounded by dignitaries as he proclaims the first Jubilee of 1300 from the Loggia of the Basilica. The work is attributed to Giotto, who is believed to have made the pilgrimage to Rome in that year.

The Orsini Chapel, Greek cross in form, is the work of Galilei and has, on the left, the tomb and bronze statue of Clement XII.

The ambulatory, with memorial tablets and monuments, leads to the sacristy. On either side of the sacristy door, the *Tabula Mater Lateranensis*, two ancient inscriptions in mosaic. Connected to the sacristy, the small chapel of the relics, with a Giottesque fresco of *St. Anne, the Madonna and Child*. In a glass case is the chair of Pius V.

From the church we enter the cloister, a tremendous accomplishment by the Roman marble-worker Pietro Vassalletto and his son, built between 1222 and 1230 by order of Honorius II and Gregory IX. The cloister is square, enclosed by loggias ornamented by small coupled columns, some twisted, some smooth, some encrusted with mosaics, as is the frieze. In the center of the cloister garden is a well dating back to Pascal I (817). Under the portico, to the right, is the bronze door ordered by

Above: apse of the Basilica
ancient papal throne

Celestine III in 1196. Beyond the door are fragments of the early basilica, the remains of the episcopal chair, altar and ciborium, tombstones, inscriptions, frescoes and other interesting artifacts. To the right of the presbytery is the door of the basilica's lateral façade, by Fontana. It is composed of two porticoes surmounted by five arches. Above the door and set slightly back is an earlier construction, comprising a central part flanked by two belltowers, commissioned by Pius IV and bearing his coat of arms. The 16th-century façade, severe and simple in its use of Ionic and Corinthian orders, has a spacious air and the cusps of the two small belltowers silhouetted against the sky lighten the entire structure. The portico contains a bronze statue of Henry IV of France, by Cordier.

The lateral façade opens on to a square in which stands a granite Egyptian obelisk, the tallest in Rome (140 feet, including the pedestal).

Below: Interior of the Baptistry.

Baptistery of St. John Lateran

The baptistery is to the right of the side entrance to the basilica. It was built by Constantine over the baths of his villa and restored by Sixtus III after an earthquake, around 432. For a long time it was the only baptistery in Rome and came to be used as a model for other baptisteries. Octagonal, it is rich in colored and gilded marble. Eight porphyry columns support the achitrave,

95

on which rest eight white marble columns supporting the internal walls of the building. In the center is a large green basalt basin in which, according to legend, Constantine was baptized.

The chapels at each side of the entrance were built under St. Hilary in the 5th century and dedicated to St. John the Baptist and St. John the Evangelist. When the bronze doors of the former are opened and closed, harmonious sounds are heard.

Facing the entrance is the chapel of St. Seconda and St. Rufina, with a very beautiful apsidal mosaic from the 5th century and, on the door, a crucifix from the school of Andrea Bregno.

To the left of the side entrance is the Lateran Palace, originally the *patriarchio*, or popes' residence, from the time of Constantine to the Avignonese emigration.

The present palace is the work of Fontana. Today it is the seat of the Cardinal Vicar and of the Curia of the Roman Diocese. Until a few years ago it also housed the Lateran Museums, containing classical pagan and Christian art. These collections are now in the Vatican.

Above: the Holy-Stairs composed of 28 marble steps covered with wood.

Holy Staircase

The flight of steps is a short distance from the basilica of St. John Lateran. Tradition says that St. Helen, the mother of Constantine, had the steps brought from Pontius Pilate's palace in Jerusalem, and that Jesus had walked up them on the day of His Passion.

The Scala Santa has 28 marble steps

Below: Facade of the basilica of St. Paul's Outside the Walls.

covered with wood to protect them from being worn down by the faithful, who climb them on their kness. At the foot of the steps are two marble groups, *The Kiss of Judas* and *Ecce Homo*, by Ignazio Jacometti.

At the top of the Scala Santa and the four other flights of stairs which are on either side of it is the Chapel of St. Lawrence Martyr. Through a grating can be seen the interior of the chapel, called *Sancta Sanctorum* because of the many relics it contains. This is the papal chapel from the original Lateran Palace, reconstructed as part of the Scala Santa by Föntana in the 16th century, under Sixtus V.

Basilica of St. Paul

This is the largest church in Rome after St. Peter's. Some of the meetings of the Ecumenical Council were held here, as if Paul VI desired the blessing of the Apostle who was the moving force behind the expansion of the primitive, undivided church. Nor should it be forgotten that it was here, on January 25, 1959, that another pope, the beloved John XXIII, gave the first announcement of the Second Vatican Ecumenical Council, which was to open a new Pentecostal age for the church. This basilica is one of the four major churches erected by Constantine (314), over the *cella memoriae* of St. Paul. It was later enlarged by Valentinian II (386), Theodosius, and Honorius V (5th century). The triumphal arch with

Basilica of St. Paul's
Outside the Walls:
Above, on the right two
details of the splendid
mosaic of the apse;
below, detail of the
candelabra executed by
Nicola d'Angelo and
Pietro Vassalletto in 1170.

magnificent mosaics from the tomb of Galla Placidia (5th century) is all that remains intact from the primitive basilica, almost entirely destroyed by fire the night of July 15, 1823. The reconstruction, following the original design, was begun by Leo XII and carried out by the architects Belli, Bosio, Camporesi and Poletti. The new building was consecrated by Pius IX in 1854. A majestic, four-sided portico of 150 columns, with a statue of St. Paul, by Canonica, in the center of the portico, precedes the main façade which overlooks the Tiber.

On the façade, which is Basilical in style, are the large mosaics *Christ with St. Peter and St. Paul, Agnus Dei, and Four Prophets.* The center door is bronze; the door on the right is the Porta Santa.

The interior is bathed in a diffused light from the alabaster windows; the solemn, severe majesty of the building makes us pause and reflect for a moment before the mortal remains of one who saw the Gospel as an ecumenical announcement. The five naves are divided by 80 granite columns. Above the columns, running around the center nave, are mosaic likenesses of the popes, beginning with St. Peter. Between the windows are modern frescoes depicting the life of St. Paul. At the sides of the central door are four alabaster columns given to Gregory VI by the Viceroy of Egypt. *Christ Blessing with the Evangelists and the 24 Venerable Men* of the Apocalypse dominate the basilica from above the triumphal arch. Below, the likenesses of St. Peter and St. Paul.

The high altar has a Gothic tabernacle by Arnolfo da Cambio. Beneath the

Above: Papal Altar of the Basilica of St. Paul, in which the body of the Apostle is kept.

Upper Section (opposite page) Triumphal Arch of Galla Placidia e Abside.

Right: the cloister of the Benedictine monastery beside the Basilica.

altar in the Confession lies the body of the Apostle, whose head, along with that of St. Peter, is preserved in the Lateran basilica.

In the right arm of the transept is the beautiful Easter candlestick by Vassalletto. The apsidal mosaics are Venetian (1220).

To the left of the apse are the splendid Chapel of St. Stephen and the Chapel of the Crucifix. The latter contains a crucifix which is said to have spoken to St. Bridget. To the right of the apse are the Chapel of St. Lawrence, with a 14th-century crucifix, and the Chapel of St. Benedict, with twelve Roman columns from Veio. At the far end of the right arm of the transept is a mosaic by Giulio Roman, from a design by Raphael, depicting the *Coronation of the Virgin*.

Passing through the sacristy we reach the harmonious cosmatesque cloister enclosed by a portico of coupled columns (Vassalletto, 1193-1214). The museum of the basilica contains the bronze door of the early basilica (11th century); in the basilica library is the Bible of Charles the Bald.

It should be noted here that the martyrdom of the Apostle did not occur here on the Via Ostiensis, but (according to tradition) a few miles farther on, on the Via Laurentina, at a spot known as the Acquae Salvie. Three churches were built there in his memory: Sts. Vincent and Anastasius (7th century), which today is in the charge of Trappist monks; Santa Maria in Scala Coeli, rebuilt by Della Porta in 1582; and San Paolo alle Tre Fontane, from the 5th century, also rebuilt by Della Porta. In this last church are the three springs

Perspective view
of the central nave.

The Chapel
altar.

which burst forth at the points touched
by St. Paul's rolling head after he was
decapitated. In one corner of the
church is the column to which he was
tied for the execution.

Basilica of St. Mary Major

The dedication of one of the four major
basilicas of Rome to the Madonna is a
sign of the devotion in which she has
always been held by the Church. She
has been, throughout Christianity, the
model for the Church itself, the most
natural and direct way to Christ.
The antiquity of the basilica proves
that even in the early days of Christianity the Marian cult was very strong.
The proclamation of the dogmas of the
Immaculate Conception (Pius IX, 1854)
and the Assumption (Pius XII, 1950)
added two small jewels to the crown of
glory which honors Holy Mary, blessed
among women, chosen by Providence
to be the Mother of God.
The Madonna is venerated here under
the name of *Salus Populi Romani* to
commemorate her as a symbol of faith
and hope during the tragic days of the
recent past.
The church is also known as the Basilica Liberiana, because according to
tradition the Madonna appeared to
Pope Liberius and a nobleman, Giovanni, on the night of August 5, 352,
ordering them to build a church on the
spot in which snow would be found the
following day. Historically, however,
the church was founded by Sixtus III in
433 on the Esquiline Hill. In the 12th
and 14th centuries the portico was add-

ed, the belltower built and the tribune enlarged. The Romanesque belltower is the tallest in Rome. The façade is by Ferdinando Fuga. who received the commission from Benedict XIV. There are five doorways in the façade, the next to the last one on the left being the Porta Santa. In the loggia, entered by the last door on the left, are the priceless mosaics from the old façade depicting the vision of Liberius. The interior still has the harmonious aspect of the old basilica, Latin cross in form. The three naves are divided by forty monolithic columns. The pavement of the central nave is cosmatesque (12th century); the gilded wood ceiling is from the early 16th century and is attributed to Giuliano Sangallo. The mosaics running above the columns tell the stories of Abraham, Isaac and Jacob, and the mosaics of the triumphal arch (5th century) show scenes from the infancy of Christ.

Facade of the Basilica with the loggia of the Benediction.

The Sistine Chapel seen from the outside.

The canopy, by Fuga, is supported by four porphyr columns. In the Confession is a statue of Pius IX kneeling. The high altar contains the relics of the Apostle Matthew and of other martyrs. In the apse is the stupendous mosaic by Jacopo Torriti (1295) of the *Triumph of the Virgin*. The exterior of the apse, the two cupolas of the Sistine and Pauline chapels and the flight of steps leading to the Piazza dell'Esquilino are by Carlo Rainardi (1673). In the right nave is found the baptistery by Flaminio Ponzi with a baptismal font by Valadier (1825) and a statue of the *Assumption* by P. Bernini (1610).

The sacristy is also the work of Flaminio Ponzio. Next to it is the Chapel of the Relics. Among the relics are

Basilica of Santa Maria Maggiore:
Details of the two
beautiful mosaics
that decorate the central nave.
*Above: the nobleman Giovanni
and Pope Liberio.*
*Right: The separation
of Abraham and Lot.*

St. Joseph taken from the
Nativity Scene by
Arnolfo di Cambio.

The bas relief of the
« Adoration of the Magi »
found in the apse.

fragments of Jesus' cradle, which on
Christmas night are carried in procession
and venerated at the altar of the
Confession. On the back wall is the
Sistine Chapel, a harmonious work by
Fontana, with frescoes of the Old and
New Testaments dating from the end
of the 16th century. In the chapel are
monuments to Sixtus V and Pius V.

At the far end of the left nave is the
Pauline Chapel (also known as the
Borghesiana) commissioned by Paul V
and built by Flaminio Ponzio; this is
considered to be the most beautiful
chapel in the world.

On the right wall of the chapel is the
monument to Clement VIII by Silla
Davidgin; on the left wall is the monument
to Paul V Borghese by the same
sculptor.

The cupola's frescoes are by Cavalier
d'Arpino and Cigoli. The Byzantine
likeness of the Virgin, on the high altar,
is among the oldest in Rome and today
is venerated with the name *Salus Populi
Romani,* as was mentioned above

OTHER CHURCHES

The tombs of the martyrs are the true great treasure of Rome. A visit to the churches or other spots sanctified by the martyrs is a personal appeal to the Christian conscience. For this reason visiting a church dedicated to a martyr cannot be considered the same as sight-seeing on the Palatine Hill or walking through the Forum. Such a visit must be the occasion for a personal encounter from which will spring self-renewal. To mention all the churches in Rome would be impossible: it would require several volumes. The pilgrim must necessarily limit himself to visiting those which are considered the most important and of most historical interest.

In ancient Rome there were 25 titular churches (somewhat akin to parish churches) in addition to seven, and later 14, regional deaconships and six Palatine deaconships.

These two types of ministry, together with that of the seven suburbicarian bishops, were the origin of the College of Cardinals, who not only elected the pope, but also acted as counsellors and collaborators. Even when, in the 12th century, cardinal bishops were created whose residences were outside of Rome they were always connected with a *titolus*, or church within the city, to point up the fact that the presbyters of Rome were the original electors of Peter's successor and, in addition, testified to the close collaboration between the Cardinals and the Popes.

SAN LORENZO FUORI LE MURA (St. Lawrence Outside the Walls). To St. Lawrence, the great deacon of the Roman Church, many beautiful churches have been dedicated, commemorating some circumstance of his life and martyrdom. Thus, St. Lawrence in Panisperna rises on the spot where he died, St. Lawrence in Fonte, where he was imprisoned, St. Lawrence in Lucina marks the location of a house in hich he was often a guest, St. Lawrence in Miranda the place where he was judged and condemned to death.

The body of the most illustrious deacon of Rome, who suffered martyrdom by fire under Valerian on August 10, 258, was buried on Via Tiburina in Agro Verano, the property of the family of Ciriaca, a Christian widow. The martyr could not be buried in one of the cemeteries of the Roman Church, because of their confiscation by the emperors. His sepulchre very soon attracted pilgrims, since St. Lawrence had become the symbol of the victory of Rome over paganism. His feast day, the most solemn of all feast days, held first place after that of Sts. Peter and Paul.

Several basilicas were erected over the tomb of the martyr. Constantine ordered one built, to which were later added the *Basilica Maior*, the *Basilica ad corpus* of Pelagius II (370-390) and the Basilica of Honorius III (1216-1227). This latter is the one in existence today, being more impressive than ever after the terrible bombing of July 19, 1943, during which Pius XII came to give comfort to the wounded.

The interior of the basilica, with 22 antique Ionian columns in granite supporting the architraves, the monumental cosmatesque pulpits of the 12th and 13th centuries, the presby-

tery's 12 unaligned Corinthian columns, the characteristic *matroneum* and the marvelous pontifical chair covered with mosaics, seems to be the perfect place to withdraw from the world in prayer.

PANTHEON (The Pantheon). Built in 27 B.C. by Agrippa and restored by Domitian after the fire of 80 A.D., the Pantheon is the best preserved of all the monuments of ancient Rome. After it had again suffered damage, it was rebuilt in its present form by Hadrian in 130 A.D. The temple is composed of a *pronaos* leading to a large circular chamber covered by a cupola. In 609 Boniface IV consecrated it as a Christian church, dedicating it to the Virgin and the Martyrs with the name of SANCTA MARIA AD MARTYRES.

The perfectly proportioned church is entered through a bronze portal. The large circular space is covered by a coffered cupola with height and diameter of approximately 132 feet. There is a large circular opening at the summit of the cupola.

In the first niche to the right is a lovely *Annunciation*, attributed to Antoniazzo Romano.

Buried in the Pantheon are the first two kings of Italy and the first queen, as well as other important personages and artists such as Raphael and Arcangelo Corelli.

SANTA PRASSEDE (St. Praxid). The *Titulus Praxedis* is first mentioned in an epitaph dated 401 and found in the cemetery of Ippolito on Via Tiburina. The church was probably located in the *Vicus Lateranus.* The present reconstruction was ordered by Pascal I, who endowed it with a large number of relics of the martyrs, removed from ruined suburban cemeteries. These holy relics preserved in the crypt under the presbytery, together with the early Christian memories the church evokes and its priceless monuments make St. Praxid a church of great importance. Among the various works of art is the Chapel of St. Zeno, the mausoleum of Theodora, the

mother of Pascal I. The chapel is also thought to contain the tombs of several popes.

The exterior of the church has black granite columns with Ionic capitals from the 6th century, a beautiful portal and mosaics of the *Madonna and Child, Praxid and Prudentia, Christ with the Apostles and Other Saints.* The interior has been defined as the Garden of Paradise because of the lovely mosaics and the varicolored marble of the pavement, an ancient example of *opus sectile.* The triumphal arch with 9th-century mosaics is contemporary with the Chapel of St. Zeno.

SANTA PRUDENZIANA (St. Prudentia). The church was constructed by Pope Silicius (384-399) on the spot where, according to tradition, rose the house of the senator, Pudens, St. Peter's host from 41 to 50 A.D. Prudentia and her sister Praxid, along with their father, were converted by St. Peter. Of the ancient romanesque facade remain the two columns and the lintel of the main door, as well as the belltower (12th century). Worthy of notice is the mosaic of the semidome (4th century), which portrays the *Redeemer Among the Apostles and the Sisters Prudentia and Praxid.*

SAN MARTINO AI MONTI (St. Martin's of the Hills). On the ruins of Trajan's baths Pope Sylvester I (314-335) founded the *Titolus Equizii* where, in the presence of Constantine, he held the preliminary meetings for the Council of Nicaea (325). Simmacus (498-514) enlarged the structure by adding the church dedicated to St. Martin, Bishop of Tours, who was highly venerated in the early years of Christianity. Later, the *Titulus Silvestri* succeeded to the *Titulus Equizii.*

Among the various popes who modified the building Sergius II should be especially remembered. Its titular pastor for twenty-years he reconstructed the church entirely, enriching it with numerous relics of the martyrs which had been found in the catacombs and dedicating it to the Sts.

Sylvester and Martin.
Nothing remains of the primitive structure except some ruins lying underneath the present building.

SAN PIETRO IN VINCOLI (St. Peter in Chains).

Also called the Eudoxian Basilica because it was built by order of the Empress Eudoxia, mother of Ventinian III, in 422, for the veneration of the chains which bound St. Peter. Rebuilt by Sixtus IV in 1475, it was restored in the 18th century. The facade is preceded by a portico. The majestic interior contains as its most important work the *Moses* of Michelangelo (1513), from the mausoleum of Julius II. Originally the work undoubtedly had quite different proportions: the *Moses* is the only remaining statue of the 44 intended for the church, the others having found their way into various museums. The figures at each side of Moses, Rachel and Leah, were begun by Michelangelo but finished, as was the rest of the church, by his pupils. Beneath the high altar, in a bronze tabernacle with reliefs attributed to Caradosso (1477) are the chains which bound the wrists of St. Peter.
In the left nave is a *Deposition* by Pomarancio. The altar over which it is hung takes its name from this painting.

SAN VITALE.

San Vitale was a Roman martyr (erroneously confused with one of the same name from Ravenna) whose house was probably located on this spot. The church was first called San Vitale during the pontificate of Gregory the Great, who had proclaimed that widows' processions should start from here. The primitive church, with three naves, was erected as a *titulus* by Innocent I (402-517). Like many other churches it has undergone modification and restoration. The old facade, one of the few structures remaining from the 5th century, was recently restored. San Giovanni Fischer, named Cardinal by Paul III in 1535, was titular pastor of San Vitale. He was later martyred for the faith.

The Pantheon, ancient pagan temple, now dedicated to the Madonna.

The basilica of San Lorenzo Outside the Walls.

SANTA SUSANNA. The ancient *Titulus Caii,* dedicated to St. Gavinius and St. Susanna, brother and niece of the sainted Pope Caius. The persecutions of Diocletian, violent and of long duration as they were, could not prevail against the faith of martyrs such as these three. Another great martyr is buried here: Felicitas, mother of seven martyred sons. St. Augustine wrote a beautiful laud in honor of this extraordinary family, which suffered martyrdom under Marcus Aurelius.

The devotion shown by the Roman Church to Felicitas and her sons is demonstrated by the fact that they were remembered in four seasonal masses. They were highly venerated by St. Damaso, St. Boniface I, St. Peter Chrysologus and St. Gregory the Great.

SANTA MARIA IN DOMNICA. This is the oldest deaconship in Rome and its titular pastor is the first cardinal deacon. Constructed over the ruins of a Roman house, it was rebuilt by Pascal I in 847 and later by the future Leo X in the 16th century. The façade is preceded by a portico of five arcades, by Sansovino. In the interior, the triumphal arch and apse are decorated with mosaics from the time of Pascal I.

SAN GIOVANNI E PAOLO (St. John and Paul). These two saints were martyrs during the reign of Julian the Apostate. Julian's insane desire to restore paganism was answered by the loyalty and faith of these martyrs. His bestial hatred was answered by the charity of John and Paul who spoke thus to the ministers of the persecutor: « If your master is Julian, make your peace with him. We have no other master but our Lord Jesus Christ ».

The church was built on the spot where a contemporary of John and Paul, a senator, Bisante, was martyred. His son San Pannachio, a friend of St. Jerome, also met martyrdom there, as did Crispin, Crispinian, and Benedict. Shortly afterward, their executioner Terenziano and his son met the same fate on the same spot.

The church was the *titulus* of many famous popes: Honorius III, Innocent VI, Hadrian VI, Leo XI and Paul V. The romanesque belltower, the portico and the external gallery of the apse are from the 12th century. The three-naved interior was completely restored by Cardinal Paolucci in 1718. To the right is the beautiful chapel, Greek cross in form, dedicated to St. Paul of the Cross, the founder of the Passionists, who are in charge of the church.

Beneath the church is the home of the two martyrs, a rare example of a two-storied Roman house. There are also about twenty rooms belonging to three buildings from both the pagan and Christian eras. The Christian frescoes are similar to those usually found in the catacombs, with the fish (a symbol of Christ expressed with the Greek word whose letters form the initials of the basic formula of the faith: Jesus Christ, Son of God the Savior), the dove and the orante. This latter, stands with arms outspread and eyes lifted to Heaven, according to the usage of the early Christians.

SAN CLEMENTE (St. Clement). St. Clement, with its relics of the martyr, its thousand-year old history and its famous frescoes, creates a strong impression, one which is also felt in the *mitreum,* the subterranean sanctuary of Mithras, over which the church is built.

Dedicated to the third pope after St. Peter, the building is actually two churches, one on top of the other. In 1108, Pascal II rebuilt the earlier basilica, which had been erected in the 5th century on ruins dating from the Republican and Imperial eras. The three naves of the church are divided by 16 Roman columns; the pavement is cosmatesque. The relics of the saint are in the crypt. The lower basilica, which was known to St. Jerome, is reached through the sacristy. In the vestibule are frescoes of the life of St. Clement, painted from the 6th to the 12th century. In the center nave are frescoes from the middle of the 9th century; in the right nave a *Madonna and Child* in the Byzantine style.

SAN MARCELLINO E PIETRO (Sts. Marcellin and Peter).

The titular saints, Marcellin the priest and Peter the exorcist, were martyrs under Diocletian. Their bodies were buried on Via Cornelia, where they remained until 826, when they were secretly taken to France and later to Germany. Constantine's mother, St. Helen, built the basilica in their honor. The observance of the Stations of the Cross took place here, with Pope Gregory the Great giving the homily of the third Saturday of Lent. After the church had been restored by several popes, it was completely rebuilt by Benedict XIV, who had been its titular pastor.

SAN GREGORIO MAGNO (St. Gregory the Great).

Originally, the church was erected on the property of the *gens Anicia*, whose last great descendant was Gregory the Great. He transformed the building into a convent and dedicated it to St. Andrew. One almost feels the presence here of the powerful figure of that great pope whose lifetime saw both the end of Roman power which ushered in the Dark Ages and the birth of a new empire and a new Rome.

He was an extraordinary example of both grandeur and humility. On the one hand he intrepidly confirmed the primacy of Rome in the Christian world and on the other he humbly proclaimed himself the « servant of the servants of God ». During his reign Christianity spread throughout Europe, England was converted, heresies were dissolved by the teachings of this mystic doctor of the church, and not least of all, the laws of ecclesiastical music were fixed.

The church was rebuilt by Gregory II and dedicated to its founder; it was restored in 1725. The campanile rises from constructions of the Claudian era. The façade, built by the order of Cardinal Scipione Borghese in 1633, is preceded by a cloistered courtyard with a portico. The interior, basilical in form, has three naves; it was completely renewed in the 18th century. The naves are divided by 16 different antique columns, flanked by pilasters. At the back, to the right, is the small room of the sainted pope with the bishop's chair and the stone which served him as a bed.

Worth noting are the ancient pulpit and the candelabrum from the 15th century, the cosmatesque choir (12th century), the bishop's chair which is carved with parts of the 23rd homily delivered by St. Gregory. The mosaic of the triumphal arch, a *Transfiguration*, goes back to Leo III.

Alongside the church are the three oratories of St. Andrew, (with frescoes by Domenichino and Guido Reni), St. Sylvia and St. Barbara. In the latter is the table from which St. Gregory served bread to the poor.

SANTI QUATTRO CORONATI (The Four Crowned Saints).

This church commemorates two martyrdoms, that of the five sculptors from Pannonia who were martyred because they refused to make a statue of Aesculapius, and that of four Roman soldiers, Severius, Severian, Carpoforus and Victorin, who refused to worship it. The basilica is dedicated to the soldiers.

The building goes back to the 4th century and is surrounded by a wall with a squat belltower. In the 12th century it was rebuilt by Pascal II. The interior has three naves and a cosmatesque pavement from the 13th century. The coffered wood ceiling is from the 16th century. On the walls are 13th-century frescoes and in the apse are other frescoes figuring the lives of the titular saints.

The cloister (13th century) is entered from the left nave and is one of the finest examples of Roman marble work in existence. In the center of the cloister is the *labrum* (a fountain for ablutions) of Pascal II.

In the portico which separates the two courtyards is the oratorio of St. Sylvester. It has 13th-century frescoes, in the Byzantine style, illustrating the *Legend of Constantine*.

SANTO STEFANO ROTONDO (St. Stephen Rotondo).

This is one of the oldest churches in Italy and the largest circular church in the world.

Although it is possible that it was erected over a pre-existing Roman building (probably in the center of the market-place), it may have been a Christian church from its origin. Consecrated by St. Simplicius at the time of Odoacer, it is composed of three concentric rings, transected by four naves in the shape of a Greek cross. The restorations of Nicolo V, which closed the outer ring and three arms of the Greek cross, considerably reduced the perimeter of the building.

The interior has 56 granite columns. To the left is a large wooden tabernacle and the episcopal chair of Gregory the Great. In the only remaining arm of the cross is the Chapel of the Sts. Primus and Felician, which has an apsidal mosaic from the 7th century representing the Crucifixion. On the walls are frescoes by Tempesta and Pomarancio with horrifying *Scenes of Martyrdom*.

SAN SISTO VECCHIO. This was the most important church on the Appian Way in the 5th century and among the most important *titula* of the Roman Church, as well as a very ancient Lenten station (the stations were held on Sunday, Wednesday and Friday). The church was reconstructed by Innocent III: the outside walls, part of the apse and the belltower date from that time. Nothing remains of the primitive church. The most important memory honored here

is that of Domenico Guzmann, who, becoming a *civis romanus*, absorbed many monasteries into his order.

SAN GIOVANNI A PORTA LATINA (St. John at the Porta Latina). At the Porta Latina, facing the Alban Hills, the Church wished to perpetuate the memory of the martyrdom to which the Apostle John was condemned by Domitian. It was here that he responded affirmatively to Christ's question, « Are you able to receive the baptism which I will receive? » The octagonal chapel of San Giovanni in Oleo, redone by Borromini, and the lovely three-naved basilica, recently restored, date from the 5th century, while the belltower is from the 16th century. The arrangement of the arches and vaults, the frescoes suffused with the calm light filtered through the large golden onyx inserts of the apse make the visitor feel the mystic presence of the disciple most loved by Christ.

SANTI NEREO E ACHILLEO (Sts. Nereus and Achilleus). The church dates back to the 4th century but was rebuilt by Leo III in 800 and restored much later by Cardinal Baronio. It was originally called *Titulus Fasciolae* because, tradition says, St. Peter, escaping from the Mamertine prison lost on this spot the bandages covering the wounds from the chains on his wrists.

The harmonious facade of
Santa Maria in Domnica.

A view of the church
of San Clemente.

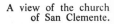

SANT'ANDREA AL QUIRINALE
(*St. Andrew at the Quirinal*). This
church combines rich works of art
(it was known as the Jewel of the
Baroque) and the vivid memory of
virtue such as that of St. Stanislaus
Kostka (a Jesuit who died when he
was barely eighteen years old) and
Charles Emanuel IV, King of Sarde-
gna and Piedmont, who, after having
abdicated, became a religious and
died here. It is one of Borromini's
finest works. The facade is Corinthian; the interior elliptical, is elegant
and rich. Particularly worthy of at-
tention are the tabernacle and the
engraved urn of St. Stanislaus and
the statue of *St. Andrew in Glory*,
sculpted by Raggi from a design by
Bernini.

SANTA MARIA DEGLI ANGELI
(*St. Mary of the Angels*). Constructed in 1563 by commission of Pius IV,
the church was transformed from the
tepidarium of Diocletian's baths by
Michelangelo. In 1749 it was redone
by Vanvitelli. The church is now
used for official ceremonies.
The interior, Greek cross in form, is
spacious, especially in the transept,
whose vault rests on eight monolithic
columns of red granite which were
formerly in the baths. The remaining
columns are of masonry.
On the walls are large paintings,
among which are *St. Jerome and
Other Saints*, by Muziano; the *Mass
of St. Basil*, by Subleyras; the *Fall*

of *Simon the Magician*, by Batoni;
the *Martyrdom of St. Sebastian*, by
Domenichino; the *Baptism of Christ*,
by Maratta. In the transept is a
statue of St. Bruno, founder of the
Carthusians, done in 1766 by G. A.
Houdon, who said to Clement XIV,
« If it weren't for the rule of silence,
this statue would speak ».
Among the tombs of important personages is that of Pius IV, from a
design by Michelangelo.

SANTA COSTANZA (*St. Constance*).
The church is circular with a cupola
erected on 24 columns. It was built
by Constantine in the 4th century as
a mausoleum for his daughters Constance and Helen and transformed
into a church in 1250. The mosaics
of the two side apses are from the
5th and 7th centuries. They depict
(on the left), *The Redeemer with St.
Peter and St. Paul* and on the right,
The Consignation of the Keys.
Around the cupola are Christian
mosaics from the 4th century.

SANT'ANASTASIA (*St. Anastasia*).
This venerable basilica was formerly
called *Titulus Anastasiae* (or Anastasis) and was built at the foot of the
hills of the Caesars at one of the
most sacred spots of paganism, to
celebrate the Passion and Resurrection of Christ. In fact the word
Anastasis brings to mind the powerful force of the One who, conquering death with his Resurrection gave

Arcades of the church
of the Santi Quattro Coronati.

The beautiful campanile
of San Giovanni e Paolo.

the victory prize to the world. In this church are kept the seven crosses which are carried in front of the seven groups of clergy, corresponding to the seven ecclesiastical regions.

SAN GIORGIO IN VELABRO (*St. George in Velabro*). Since the authentic records of his martyrdom have been lost, little is known of this saint except that he was from the Orient. The church was built in the 6th century on the ruins of the Foro Boario and was rebuilt by Leo II in 682. The portico, the marble frieze and the belltower are from the 12th century.

SS. COSMA E DAMIANO (*Sts. Cosma and Damian*). The church was built in 527 by Pope Felix IV, in a hall of the Forum of Peace, and restored in 1632 from designs by Arrigucci. A circular temple to the God Romolus serves as a vestibule for the church.
The interior has fine mosaics from the 6th century, both on the triumphal arch and in the apse, with *Jesus Among Sts. Peter, Paul, Cosma, Damian, Theodore and Felix IV*. The ceiling (1632) has reliefs of the coat of arms of Urban VIII.

SANTA FRANCESCA ROMANA (*St. Frances Romana*). The church was built in the 10th century and has often been restored. The facade is by C. Lombardi (1615). On the high altar is a *Madonna and Child*, in Byzantine style, from the 12th century. In the center of the Confession (Bernini, 1640) is a statue of *St. Francis and an Angel*, by Meli (1866). Beneath the Confession is the crypt with the tomb of the titular saint. In the semidome of the apse is a mosaic, *The Virgin and Four Saints* (12th century).
Behind a protecting iron gate, in the right arm of the transept, are two stones from the Via Sacra with imprints which legend says were left by St. Peter when he knelt to pray God to punish Simon the Magician by interrupting his sacrilegious flight (it seems that the church was built on the spot where Simon fell). Still in the right arm of the transept is a monument to Gregory XI (1378) by Olivieri, erected in 1584 by the Romans in gratitude to the Pope who had brought the papacy back from Avignon. Figured in basrelief is the pope entering Rome by the Porta San Paolo with St. Catherine of Siena by his side. In the sacristy, among other paintings, are *Santa Maria Nova* (on wood, 5th century) and the *Miracle of St. Benedict*, an altar frontal by Subleyras (1744).

SANTA MARIA ANTIQUA. The church was built in the 6th century, transforming what was presumed to be the library of Augustus at the foot of the Palatine. It is of historical importance, being the oldest example of the transformation of a pagan building into a Christian edifice. Byzantine frescoes form its decoration and date from the 7th and 8th centuries. Among their subjects are the *Teoria dei Santi* and *The Adoration of the Cross* (in the apsidal semidome) and *The Crucifixion*.

SAN LUCA E MARTINA. This church consists of two structures, one on top of the other. It is located in front of the Mamertine Prison. The lower one, which was built in the 6th century, occupies the place of the former « secretarium senarus ». It was dedicated to St. Martina. At street level, the façade of the upper one overlooks the Roman Forum. It is dedicated to St. Luke and is the work of Pietro da Cortona.

S. MARIA D'ARA COELI. This church was built on the hill of Campidoglio which was the site of the Rock of Citadel of Rome. Its name is due to the legend which says that in this place, the birth of Jesus Christ was foretold to Augustus by the Sibyl. It was built in the 5th century, and in 1250 it passed from the Benedictines to the Franciscans, who enlarged it. The large staircase of 124 steps was built by the Romans in 1348 for having been saved from the plague.
The interior is made up of three

naves divided by 22 columns. The floor is cosmatesque of the 13th century. A chapel offered by Nicolò Bufalini is in the nave on the right. Here there are frescoes representing the « Life of St. Bernardino » by Pinturicchio and the « Stigmas of St. Francis » (1485). At the back of the middle nave, there are two pulpits which belonged to Lorenzo and Giacomo Costa, dating back to about 1200. On the high altar there is a painting of the Madonna from the 12th century in Byzantine style. The chapel dedicated to St. Helena is in the center of the left transept. It has eight columns and a porphyritic urn. This chapel, according to tradition, is located in the same place in which Augustus erected an altar after the Sibyl's prophecy. In the back of the transept, there is a fresco « Madonna on the Throne with the Child and Saints » by Cavellini. In a small chapel in the sacristy the « Holy Child » is kept, a small statue venerated by the Roman people.

SAN MARCO. The basilica, founded by the pope St. Mark in 336, was reconstructed almost completely in 833 by Gregory IV. The arch of triumph and the apse were decorated with mosaics. Among the various works of art are two painting by Melozzo da Forlì, « St. Mark the Pope » and « St. Mark the Evangelist », and a « Tabernacle » from the 15th century by Mino da Fiesole in the sacristy.

BASILICA DEI SANTI APOSTOLI. The basilica was probably built in 1560 by Pelagio I, in honor of St. Giacomo in Minore and St. Philip. It was greatly restored by Martin V and by the pontiffs of the Della Roveri family, and was almost entirely rebuilt by Carlo Fontana (1702). In the old church there was a cupola painted by Melozzo da Forlì. The remaining fragments of the cupola are kept in the Pinacoteca Vaticana. The façade, by Valadier (1827), is set back in respect to a Renaissance portico of arches by Pontelli from the 15th century. Above the portico there is a loggia around which are

the statues of Christ and the Apostles. The interior consists of three naves and is divided by big pillars. It contains various works of art. The fresco on the ceiling, the « Triumph of the Order of St. Francis » is by Fontana. At the back of the left nave, the beautiful statue of Pope Clemente XIV is by Canova. « The Ascension » by Sebastiani Ricci is on the ceiling.

SAN MARCELLO. This church, which has extremely old origins, perhaps dates back to the beginning of the 4th century. The original façade was on the side opposite the present one. In front of this original one, dramatic episodes of medieval struggles took place.
The present church is by Jacopo Sansovino, who changed the orientation. The façade is by Fontana and the statues by Francesco Cavallini. Noteworthy restorations were carried out by Virginio Vespignani in 1784. The interior, which is one rectangular nave, is in vivacious colors with a fine ceiling rich in gold. It is dedicated to the « Conception » and adorned with symbols of the Virgin (« Stella Maris, Turris davidica », etc.). In the chapels, there are valuable paintings and sculptures. In the fourth chapel on the right, the large « Crucifix » can be noted. Carved in wood, it was found intact, with the lamp still lit, among the remains of a fire in 1519.

SAN SILVESTRO IN CAPITE. This is the church of the English Catholic community. Pope Stefano III (752-57) had it built on the site of the colossal Sun Temple, erected by order of Aurelianus. The church was rebuilt in 1690. On the walls of the picturesque courtyard, which is found behind the small external façade, there are many Latin epigraphs of various origins. The name of the Church is derived from the relic of the head of St. John the Baptist, which was brought there and then preserved for many centuries.
The interior is airy and rich with six side chapels. The .fine high altar is by Rainaldi. Below it, there is

115

an elegant Confession in colored marble. The bell-tower is in cosmatesque style.

SAN CARLO AL CORSO. This large church was originally a small one dedicated to St. Ambrose. The latter was built in 1513 by the Lombardian communities on the site of the Church of St. Nicolò del Tufo, permission having been given by Sisto IV in 1471.

The present construction was begun in 1612 by Onorio Longhi and finished in 1672 by his son Martino Longhi il Vecchio. The façade is by Menicucci and Fra' Mario da Danepina. The cupola, designed by Longhi, was modified by Pietro da Cortona. The interior, in the shape of a Latin cross, consists of three naves. Among the many valuable works of art to be seen are: « Fall of the Rebellious Angels » on the ceiling of the middle nave; « Four Prophets » in the corbels of the cupola; « Glory of the Eternal Father » in the small lantern; « St. Charles in Glory » on the ceiling of the presbytery; « St. Charles Visits the Plague Stricken » on the semi-dome of the apse. All are frescoes by Brandi. On the high altar, « The Glory of St. Ambrose and St. Charles » is by Maratti.

The heart of St. Charles is kept behind the high altar in a rich reliquary. At the high altar there is also a tabernacle of the holy oil of the 15th century, which probably came from the earlier church of St. Ambrose.

SANTA MARIA DEL POPOLO (St. Mary of the People). Originally this was a small chapel which had been constructed by order of Pasquale II. Sisto IV Della Rovere ordered its complete reconstruction in 1477, which was carried out by Baccio Pontelli and Andrea Bregno.

The interior is made up of three naves and a cupola, with frescoes by Vanni, that rise above the transept. It has preserved its Renaissance character, in spite of the Baroque changes of the 18th century due to Bernini.

On the high altar is the Byzantine inspired « Madonna of the People », of the 13th century. The two colored stained glass windows are by Guglielmo di Marcillat. The frescoes that decorate the ceiling of the choir (« The Coronation of the Virgin », « The Evangelists », « The Sibyl » and « The Fathers of the Church ») are ·works of Pinturicchio. The Della Rovere Chapel (first on the right) is entirely frescoed by Pinturicchio with scenes from the life of St. Girolamo on the walls and with an altar piece representing the « Adoration of the Child ». The tabernacle of the sacristy, which contains a 14th century Madonna, was built by Bregno (1473). In the chapel to the left of the presbetery there are two masterpieces by Caravaggio: « The Conversion of St. Paul » and « The Crucifixion of St. Peter ».

In the Chigi chapel (the second on the left), there are statues of prophets in the four corners: Jonah and Eliah by Lorenzetto and Daniel and Habakkuh by Bernini. The « Birth of the Madonna » by Sebastiano del Piombo is on the altar. The mosaics of the cupola are by Luigi Di Pace (1516). They represent « God the Creator of the Firmament », with the symbols of the seven planets.

SANTA MARIA SOPRA MINERVA. This church was built on the ruins of a temple dedicated to Minerva. In 1280, it was reconstructed by the

Dominican Friars, Sisto and Ristoro. The façade is by Meo del Caprino (1453). It is the only church in Rome in Gothic style. The interior is divided into three naves by pillars which have the shape of crosses. It contains valuable works of art, especially in the noble chapels. The relics of St. Catherine of Siena, who died in Rome in 1380, are kept under the high altar. On the left of the presbetery is the famous statue, « Christ Carrying the Cross » by Michelangelo. The sacristy, frescoed by Antoniazzo Romano (1482), contains the chapel that St. Catherine died in. Cardinal Barberini ordered it brought there in 1673.

In the right wing of the transept is the Carafa Chapel, which is famous for its frescoes by Filippino Lippi. The tombstone of Beato Angelico is in the left transept.

SANT'IGNAZIO DI LOYOLA. This church was built between 1626 and 1685 according to the design of the Jesuit Orazio Grassi. The façade is by Algardi. The interior consists of three naves rich in decoration. The frescoes of the apse, of the mock cupola and of the ceiling are by the Jesuit Andrea Pozzi; the last represents the « Entrance of St. Ignatius into Paradise ». There are two large alto-relievos on the altars of the chapels of the transept: on the right, « Glory of St. Luigi Gonzaga » by Pietro Le Gros (18th century), and on the left, the « Annunciation » by Filippo Valle (18th century).

SAN LUIGI DEI FRANCESI (St. Louis of the French). This is the national French church. It was consecrated in 1580. The fine façade by Giacomo Della Porta has an upper and lower part, both of the same width. It contains frescoes by Do-menichino of episodes from the life of St. Cecilia. There are three paintings by Caravaggio relating to the « Story of St. Matthew ». The church contains tombs of famous Frenchmen.

SANT'AGOSTINO. This church was built in the 15th century by Giacomo di Pietrasanta. The façade, which is preceded by a stairway flanked with balustrades, has an upper and lower part and is in severe Renaissance style.

Among the valuable works in the interior are the « Madonna del Parto » by Sansovino, « The Prophet Isaiah » (fresco by Raphael), and the « Madonna of the Pilgrims » by Caravaggio.

SANTA MARIA DELL'ANIMA. This is the national German church (1500-1514). The bell-tower on the right side is attributed to Bramante. The « Virgin among Kneeling Figures » over the portal is attributed to Sansovino.

In the interior, among the various works, there is the monument of Hadrian VI of Utrecht, the last foreign pontiff. It was designed by Peruzzi, carried out by Nicola Tribolo, and includes the four statues « Justice », « Prudence », « Force », and « Temperance ».

SANTA MARIA DELLA PACE (St. Mary of Peace). This church was built by Sisto IV between 1480-1484. Alexander VII ordered its restoration by Pietro da Cortona, who added the Baroque façade and the semi-circular portal made up of Doric columns which precedes the façade. In the Chigi Chapel in the interior can be noted « The Sibyls » of Raphael and the central octagon which supports the cupola with Peruzzi's frescoes. The « Virgin of Peace » (or « Virgin

117

The piazza and facade of
Santa Maria in Cosmedin.

The pediment of the church
of Saint Ignatius of Loyola.

of the Miracle ») by Maderno is on the high altar. The small cloister next to the church is by Bramante.

SANT'AGNESE IN AGONE. The ferocious persecution of Decio in 250 caused the fulfillment of the desire of a sixteen year old girl to sacrifice her life for Christ. In this ancient arena Agnes was condemned to infamy for attachment to her own purity. The fame of her heroism has obscured the not negligible historical memory of the Stadium of Domitian.
The precious relic of the skull of the martyr is venerated in the church. The skull, donated by St. Pio X, was taken from her tomb in the 6th century by Honorius I so that it would be venerated near the wood of the Holy Cross in the Sancta Sanctorum of the Lateran. The church, completed by Borromini in 1657, has an interior in the shape of Greek cross and has many works of art.

SANTA MARIA IN COSMEDIN. This church was constructed in the 6th century on part of a temple dedicated to Hercules and on part of another Roman building. In the 8th century Hadrian VI was responsible for adding some ornaments. He gave the church to some Greek monks who had fled to Rome because of persecutions in the Orient. The name Cosmedin probably comes from « ornaments » (from the Greek « cosmeo »). The Romanesque bell-tower was built in the 12th century, while the church was being restored. Under the portico a mask of a fluvial divinity is sculptured, called « Bocca della Verità » (the mouth of truth). The legend says that if a guilty person put his hand in the mouth, he would be bitten. In the interior, which is divided into three naves by pillars and ancient columns there are cosmatesque works of the 12th and 13th centuries: the Schola Cantorum, the ambos, the Paschal candle, the bishop's throne. In the sacristy a mosaic of the eighth century represents « The Adoration of the Magi ».

SANTA SABINA. This church was built by Pietro di Illiria in honor of the martyred Umbrian saint and her catechist, Serapia, under the rule of Hadrian. In 122 Honorius II gave it to St. Domenico who enlarged the cloister and added the convent. The main entrance of the church has a carved wooden door of the 5th century, divided into panels representing scenes from the Old and New Testaments.

The interior is the only example in Rome of a Ravenna type Romanesque basilica of the 5th century. It is divided into three naves by 24 columns of Parian marble. The columns are made transparent by the light. In the center is the « schola cantorum », reconstructed with ancient stones, which came from the one built by Eugenio II in 824.

SANTA PRISCA. This church was already spoken of in the 5th century as Title of Prisca; later, it was certainly one of the twenty abbeys of Rome. Little credence is given to the tradition which says that the « domestica ecclesia » of Aquila and Priscilla was here where St. Peter performed his first office. An underground place dedicated to the cult of Mithras was recently discovered. It is probably the most important one due to its size, inscriptions, frescoes and records.

The attached monastery was inhabited successively by Greek, Benedictine, Franciscan and Augustinian monks. The principal restorations were those ordered by Hadrian I in 722, Callisto III in 1455, Cardinal Benedetto Giustiniani (1600) and by Clemente XII, who brought it to its present condition.

SAN SABA. This church is dedicated to the monk of Cappadòcia (439-532), martyr under the rule of Justinian. The church was rebuilt at the beginning of the 13th century.

The interior consists of three naves; the « schola cantorum » was rebuilt using ancient cosmatesque ornaments. The walls are bare and the floor is cosmatesque. The bishop's throne is kept behind the high altar. It is

The facade of the church of Sant'Agnese.

A view of San Luigi de' Francesi.

119

decorated with a fine cosmatesque frieze made of marble, with a cross. The façade is Romanesque.

SAN PAOLO ALLE TRE FONTA-NE (St. Paul at the three fountains). This church was built in the 5th century, on the site of the « Acque Salvie ». The church is built on the three legendary fountains that apparently sprang up from the ground in the places where the Apostle's decapitated head had bounced.

This place must have been unhealthy, swampy, and maybe of bad repute, too. As is known, the Disciples took the Apostle's body there where Constantine then erected the basilica, just outside the city walls. The present structure, in Ionic style, was realized by Giacomo Della Porta in 1559 and commissioned by Cardinal Pietro Aldobrandini. Noteworthy in the church are the « Crucifixion » by Guido Reni on the altar of St. Peter, the fresco representing St. Paul in front of Festo by Toschi, and the sculptures by Cordieri (Franciosino) which indicate three expressions of Paul's decapitated head.

In 1869 Pius IX ordered a wonderful mosaic, the « Four Seasons », to be transferred to this church. It was taken from a pagan temple at Ostia. Nearby is the Church of St. Vincenzo and St. Anastasio, which was probably constructed by the Byzantine Nassate and consecrated by Pope Honorius I in 625. It was rebuilt under Hadrian I and was consecrated again by Pope Honorius II in 1221. The interior, in Romanesque style, is austere and at the same time harmonious. It is well suited to the liturgy that the Trappist monks celebrate.

The church called Santa Maria Scala Coeli is also nearby. It was constructed on the site on which St. Bernard apparently had the vision, while he was celebrating Mass, of a staircase. The souls for whom he was offering the Sacrifice were ascending the stairs to heaven.

SAN BARTOLOMEO ALL'ISOLA (St. Bartholomew of the Island). This Church houses the tomb of St.

Bartholomew. It was built on the site of the temple of Esculapius on the Isola Tiberina (Island in the Tiber). The worship of God was celebrated here and flourished from the 2nd century A.D. to the 4th century.

This church was erected by the Emperor Ottone III, who was the murderer of Giovanni Crescenzio and defender of civil liberty. It recalls the struggles of the Roman people against the German emperors who came to Italy in order to impose on the Church the popes that they wanted. It was restored by Pasquale II and later destroyed by a flood in 1557. It was finally entirely rebuilt by Martino Longhi in 1624. The interior is shaped almost like an Egtian cross, with three naves divided by 14 different columns of various origins.

SANTA CECILIA. Cecilia, the holy martyr, is one of the most important Christian glories in Rome. The recognition, which was ordered in 1599 by Clemente VIII and carried out by the titular cardinal of the basilica and by Cardinal Baronio, assured Rome of the certainty of the presence of the young Roman girl's body. The fine sculpture by Maderno (who was present at the opening of the coffin) skilfully reproduced the sweet sleeping position of the uncorrupted body of the virgin. Clement VIII did not want anyone to touch the inside of the coffin and encased it in a silver tomb. The Saint, who before had been venerated by the Romans, became their beloved patron.

The church was first founded in the 5th century, on the site of the Saint's house. It was reconstructed in the 9th century by Pasquale I, who acted on an indication of the martyr in a dream. He then found the place of her sepelchure in the catacombs of San Callisto.

The bell tower and the portico were added in the 12th century. An ancient calidarium can be reached by following a corridor found at the entrance of the right nave. (It is said that in this calidarium the young girl met the martyrdom of suffocation by boiling vapors before being decapitated). The statue of the Saint, by Maderno, is under the altar. In the apse there is a precious mosaic of the 9th century, « Christ and Saints ».

The sarcophagi of St. Cecilia, St. Valeriano and other martyrs are preserved in the modern crypt in Byzantine style by Giovenale. The remains of Roman buildings of various epochs can be reached from the crypt. The precious « Redeemer » of Cavallini is in the choir of the Benedictine nuns in the monastery.

SANTA MARIA IN TRASTEVERE.

The Christian liturgy was probably officiated publicly for the first time in this place. The earlier basilica was erected by Julius I in 340. It was the first church dedicated to the Virgin.

The present basilica dates back for the most part to the era of Innocence II (1130-1143). The façade, with the Romanesque bell tower, is adorned with mosaics of the 12th and 13th centuries, representing, among other things, the « Virgin with Child » surrounded by female figures. The portico on the opposite side of the church, by Fontana, is from the beginning of the 18th century.

The interior is divided into three naves by 21 columns of various origins, with Ionic and Corinthian capitals. The « Ascensione » of Domenichino is in the center of the wooden ceiling. The floor, originally of mosaic inlay, was redone in the 19th century.

The peculiarity of the basilica is constituted by the series of mosaics which date back to the 11th century, which was a period of transition between Roman classic art and Byzantine art. The « Redeemer and Virgin surrounded by Saints » dominate a procession of sheep moving towards the cross on the semi-dome of the apse. « Isaiah and Jeremiah » is on the front of the apsidal arch.

Among the mosaics on the apsidal walls there are stories of the Virgin painted in the 13th century by Cavallini: from left to right, « The Birth of the Virgin », « The Annunciation », the « Nativity », the « Epiphany », « The Presentation to the Temple » and the « Death of the Virgin ».

SAN CRISOGONO.

This church, certainly built before 499, is one of the oldest ones in Rome. St. Crisogono was a Greek martyr killed at Grado during the persecutions of Diocletian. It is known with certainty that in the Roman council of 499, three presbyteries of the « Titulus Crisogoni » were represented. It was restored by Gregory II, the holy pope who fought against the iconoclastic emperor Leone Isaurico, and was again restored by order of Cardinal Scipione Borghese (nephew of Paul V), who erected the façade and re-did the ceiling.

The interior consists of three naves divided by 22 granite columns. Two porphyritic columns, the largest in Rome, support the principal arch. The baldachin rests on four other columns of rare alabaster. The floor is cosmatesque. A mosaic of Cavallini representing the « Virgin among St. Giacomo and St. Crisogono » is in the apse. Next to the sacristy is found the entrance to the ancient underground church. It is interesting to visit the remains of the ancient « Titulus Crisogoni », which was constructed on buildings of the Imperial Age, according to a basilican-type plan.

A monastery was built near the church, which was dedicated to St. Stephen, Lorenzo, and Crisogono. The Benedictine Order is observed. Important paintings of the 11th century can be admired in the small nave on the right.

SANT'ONOFRIO.

The church was built in 1419 and has been restored many times. It is located at the top of a flight of stairs on a panoramic terrace. There are three frescoes by Domenichino under the portico in front of the church. Scenes from the life of the Madonna frescoed by Pinturicchio and Peruzzi are in the polygonal apse.

The church of Saint Cecilia, patron of the Romans.

The façade of Sant'Andrea della Valle.

The façade of Saint Barthelomew's.

SAN PIETRO IN MONTORIO. This church was erected on the site where, according to tradition, St. Peter was crucified. It was rebuilt in the 15th century. The interior, which consists of a single nave, contains valuable works. They include the « Scourging of Christ » and other paintings of Sebastiano del Piombo, « Mary's Coronation » and the « Four Virtues » by Peruzzi. The courtyard next to the church contains the small temple of Bramante.

LA CHIESA DEL GESÙ (The Church of Jesus). This is the most important Jesuit church in Rome. It was begun in 1568 by Vignola. The façade, which represents the transition between the Renaissance and Baroque periods, was built in 1575 according to the design of Giacomo Della Porta. In the interior there are decorations with multi-colored marble, sculptures, bronzes, frescoes, and stuccos. The original fresco of Baciccia « The Triumph of the Name of Jesus » is on the ceiling. In the left transept, rising above his tomb, is the altar of St. Ignatius di Loyola, work of Andrea Pozzi. In the group of the Trinity, the terrestrial globe is the largest existing mass of lapis lazuli. At the sides of the altar there are two marble groups: « Faith » (on the left) by G. Théodon and « Religion » by Les Gros (on the right).

SANT'ANDREA DELLA VALLE. This church was begun in 1591 by Olivieri and finished in 1560 by Maderno. The majestic travertine façade is the work of Rainaldi (1665) according to the design of Maderno. The cupola, with a tambour formed by columns, is the highest in Rome after St. Peter's. The interior is in the shape of a Latin cross and has a single nave. At the extremities of the nave are the tombs of two Piccolomini popes, Pius II (died 1464) and Pius III (died 1503). Their bodies were brought here from the basilica of St. Peter in 1614. The bronze copies of Michelangelo's statues « Pieta », « Lia » and « Rachele » are in the Strozzi Chapel. Lanfranchi's frescoes on the cupola, painted between 1621 and 1625, represent the « Glory of Paradise ». « The Four Evangelists » in the corbels, the frescoes in the apse (« The Baptist indicating Jesus », « The Vocation of St. Peter and St. Andrew », « St. Andrew being led to Torture », « St. Andrew Scourged » and « St. Andrew who Ascends into Heaven »), and the six allegories of virtue, between the windows, are all by Domenichino. The three large frescoes with scenes of the « Martyrdom of St. Andrew » in the apsidal curve are by Mattia Preti (1651).

The facade of
Santa Maria in Trastevere.

SAN LORENZO IN DAMASO.
Originally this church was the large chapel of the Riario Palace (« La Cancelleria »), built by Bramante on the site of the church erected by St. Damaso in 380. This last church was in honor of St. Lorenzo and contained the archives of the Roman Church. During the French occupation (19th century), it was a stable and then a law court. It was completely restored by Valadier and then by Vespignani.
The interior preserves the singular plan of Bramante: four sides ending in an apse and surrounded by a portico which is double at the entrance and forms an inner vestibule. A baldachin of alabaster covers the high altar. The walls, the apsidal semi-dome and the beamed ceiling are full of gold.
The large frescoes of the main nave are by Fontana: « Pope Sisto II while being led to his martyrdom, predicts to St. Lorenzo that in three days he will follow him », « Pope St. Damaso with St. Girolamo receives homage from the Oriental Bishops », and the « Martyrdom of St. Lorenzo ». The famous « Crucifixion » which, according to tradition spoke to St. Brigida, is in the large chapel of the right nave. Sepulchres of cardinals and famous personages are in the churches.

The arcades of the church
of San Marco.

The famous
Trinità dei Monti.

LA CHIESA NUOVA or S. MARIA IN VALLICELLA. It was erected between the 16th and 17th centuries,

Above: façade of the church of San Giorgio in Velabro.

Left: apse of the church of San Carlo al Corso.

Right: the imposing *Moses* by Michelangelo, masterpiece by the great Florentine artist which can be admired in the church of San Pietro in Vincoli.

by Giovanni Matteo da Città di Castello and Martino Longhi il Vecchio, financed by Cardinal Cesi and supervised by St. Filippo Neri. The façade is by Fausto Rughesi.

The grand interior, with extremely rich decorations, is in the shape of a Latin cross with three naves. Pietro da Cortona frescoed it for the most part. To be noted are the splendid organs with their carvings and decorations, the choir stalls, the windows decorated in the barrel-vault. The « Virgin with St. Charles and St. Ignatius » by Maratta is on the altar in the Spada Chapel of Rainaldi, on the right of the apse. On the high altar, the « Virgin among the Angels ». To the left of the presbytery « St. Domitilla, St. Nereo and St. Archilleo ».

The mosaic of the Saint from the original painting by Guido Remi is in the chapel of St. Filippo Neri, which is to the left of the apse. The Saint rests under the altar of this chapel decorated in bronze and precious marble covered with mother-of-pearl.

In the sacristy, the statue of St. Filippo Neri is by Algardi and the ceiling is by Pietro da Cortona.

TRINITÀ DEI MONTI. This is one of the churches of the French community in Rome. It was begun by order of Charles VIII of France in 1585, consecrated by Sisto V and restored in 1816. The façade with the two symmetrical bell towers is attributed to Giacomo Della Porta. In the interior, two paintings by Daniele da Volterra: « The Deposition and « The Assumption ». The cupola is octagonal. In front of the church is the « sallustiano » obelisks, which is a Roman imitation of the Egyptian obelisks. Its construction was ordered in 1789 by Pius IV.

S. MARIA DELLA CONCEZIONE called I CAPPUCCINI. This church was built in 1624. It is noted for its underground chapels which contain earth from the Holy Land of Palestine and which are decorated with skulls and bones of thousands of monks. The painting of Guido Reni « St. Michael who overthrows the devil » is in the first chapel on the right.

SANTA CROCE IN GERUSALEM-ME (The Holy Cross in Jerusalem). This is one of the basilicas of the era of Constantine and was erected by St. Helena in 320 to house the relics brought back from the Holy Land. The church was modified several times: the most important (with the addition of the bell tower) took place in 1144 under Lucius II and transformed it into a Romanesque church. In 1743, by order of Benedict XIV, the architects Gregorini and Passalacqua changed the appearance of the church even more by adding a façade and a portal in Baroque style. The interior has the plan of a basilica with three naves divided by eight columns allied with six large pilasters. The floor is cosmatesque. On the ceiling a painting of Corrado Giaquinto (1744) depicts *St. Helena Flying to Heaven.* In the back of the apse there is a fresco of the *Finding of the Holy Cross* attributed to Antoniazzo Romano. It dates from the end of the XV century. In the chapel of the relics (left nave) there are preserved three fragments of the Cross, a nail used to crucify Our Lord, two thorns from the crown of thorns, a piece of the inscription on the cross, and the finger that St. Thomas put in Christ's side. At the beginning of the stairs (at the end of the right nave) that lead to the oldest part of the church there is the horizontal arm of the god thief Dismas' cross. The Cappella di Sant'Elena (Chapel of St. Helena), situated in the old part of the church, was built on the earth of Calvary brought to Rome by the Empress: XVI century mosaics and frescoes adorn it. On the altar there is a statue of Roman times which was found at Ostia and transformed, with the addition of the head and the hands into a likeness of St. Helena.

IMPORTANT
HISTORICAL INFORMATION

View of the
Roman Forum.

The traditional date of the founding
of Rome is 753 B.C. The founding is
attributed to Romulus, who, digging a
furrow with a plow, traced the first
boundary of the city: the rectangular
city on the Palatine hill. After him
there were seven kings of Rome. But
we have historical data beginning only
two centuries later, with the driving
out of Tarquin the Proud and the crea-

Beatissime Pater

Romam Venit
Anno Jubilei 1975
ad Apostolorum Memoriam
venerandam
et Apostolicam Benedictionem
impetrandam

sigillum   e civitate Vaticana,
                            die...

tion of a republic of aristocratic type (led by two consuls assisted by the Senate) which was made more democratic with the designation of two tribunes of the people. In spite of the class struggles that tormented it, the Roman republic consolidated itself internally and undertook those wars of conquest with the other Italic peoples, above all the Etruscans and the Samnites, which already in the II century B.C. secured it the dominion over all of Italy. Then followed the conquest of Greece and part of the Middle East. The conquest of Northern Europe begins with Julius Caesar. Caesar, who is accused of wanting to put all the power in his own hands, is killed. His heir Octavian, having defeated his political adversaries at Actium, becomes the chief of state, and after the fall of Egypt, the first Roman Emperor. He takes the title of Augustus. Under his reign in the 747th or 749th year after the foundation of Rome, Christ is born. The Roman Empire under various emperors, among whom Vespasian, Titus, Trajan, Hadrian, Marcus Aurelius, Septimus Severus, has extended in the course of three centuries all around the Mediterranean (Spain, North Africa, the Middle East, the Balkans), pushing itself as far to the north as England and Scotland. In the meantime Rome was being enriched with extremely sumptuous monuments and buildings: temples, portals, baths, gardens, circuses, fountains, and imperial and patrician palaces adorned with innumerable sculptures and paintings.

In a year not specified St. Peter arrives in Rome to found the early Christian community. Soon the persecutions begin by order of the state authorities. In

Monumental Mamertine ruins and Caesar's Forum.

Temple of Castor and Pollux.

fact, the Christians refuse to recognize the divinity of the emperors. So begins the era of the catacombs, semi-abandoned underground tunnels, in which the faithful assemble for the liturgy and for the veneration of the remains of the martyrs. In the catacombs the first Christian art is born.

In 313 Constantine, having become emperor by winning the Battle of the Milvian Bridge against his rival Massentius, grants freedom to the new cult. His successors divide the Empire into two parts, East and West. From this moment the Roman state gradually declines, above all because of the very strong pressure from the barbarians at the boundaries, until the barbarian Odacer deposes the last emperor in 476.

The city finds itself under the *de facto* rule of its Bishop, who is also the Pope. It is at the center of a succession of encounters with the barbarians that are conquering Northern Italy and the still-existing Empire of the East. There are many gaps in the historical data, and so we cannot establish with precision when the temporal power of the pope became consolidated juridically. In the first centuries of the Middle Ages the city (completely devastated and in extreme decadence by now) is prey to the fierce struggles of the patrician families. But the imperial rebirth takes place at Rome with the coronation of Charlemagne in St. Peter's Basilica on Christmas night, 800. It is indeed the pope who crowns Charlemagne as the head of the established Holy Roman Empire (composed of France, Germany, and Italy).

And it is again a pope who, after the division of the Carolingian realm, puts on the head, of Otto I of Saxony this

130

View of the Roman Forum.

Left: Temple
of Saturn.

Arch of Septimius Severus.

time, the crown of Emperor of the Holy Roman Empire (962). From this moment, however, the furious struggles between the papacy and the empire begin. These struggles last for many centuries, involving not only Rome but all of Italy, and they see the alternation of popes and antipopes until the resolving of the Western Schism (1449) the accomplishment of Nicholas V. When Pope Sixtus IV (who among other things has the Sistine Chapel built) succeeds to the Chair of St. Peter (1471), the period of the great popes of the Renaissance begins. In this period we see working in Rome Michelangelo, Raphael, Bramante, Cellini, and all the greatest artists of the age. The construction of the new St. Peter's Basilica begins. It will be consecrated in 1620 (the old church, now in ruins, was of the era of Constantine). The Vatican is also constructed in this period. The Baroque age begins, and it has precisely at Rome its greatest center of diffusion. St. Peter's and the Vatican are completed in the XVII century by Baroque artists, such as Bernini. Popes, princes, and cardinals enrich the city with art collections, palaces, villas and monumental fountains. Those constructed above all in the XVII-XVIII centuries give Rome the aspect that we admire today.

Rome becomes the capital of Italy in 1870. With national unification the kingdom of Italy is created.

Roman Forum

The Roman Forum can be considered the geographical, political, social, and religious center of ancient Rome. For

131

the whole period of classical antiquity it constitutes one of the spiritual centers of the world. It is situated among the Hills of the Palatine, the Capitol, the Esquiline, and the Celius, and is practically at the foot of what was the primitive *città quadrata* (rectangular city) on the Palatine. Originally it was a rather swampy area because it was near the Tiber River. It ceased to be a swampy area only after the first construction work, when it was reclaimed completely by the building of the *Cloaca Massima* (Great Drain), one of the most daring and colossal feats of civil engineering in antiquity. We can still see the remains of this drain on the bed of the Tiber, into which it flowed, at the height of the present Ponte Palatino.

In the lower part of the Forum along the Via Sacra we find a very ancient cemetery for the people who inhabited the near-by zones before the city was born. We can consider the Via Sacra, that crosses the entire forum uniting the Palatine with the Campidoglio (Capitol) on which it climbs, (but some consider its original length to be much longer) the natural cause of the building of the forum, because the Via Sacra made it a meeting place and above all a market for all the people living on the hills. The true forum originally consisted of a large rectangular square, a meeting place for political gatherings, public elections, business dealings, political rallies, the authentic seat of the organizing center of the *res publica*. On this square there was soon built the *Regia*, or residence of the priest-kings, the *Casa delle Vestali* (the house of the Vestals, the priestesses of the public cult who in the near-by temple guarded

Two views of the panorama of the Roman Forum.

Below: the Temple of Saturn and the Column of Phocas.

the sacred fire of the goddess Vesta), the first *Basilicas*, or halls of justice and of public ceremonies. To contemplate the Roman Forum is to contemplate the synthesis of ancient Roman history. Those who want to have a complete and organic view of it and also understand even in a very approximate way the appearance and structure of the city must climb the hill of the Capitol to the gardens at the left of the Palazzo Senatorum (the Palace of the Senate). Thus he has a distant view of the position of the imperial palaces on the Palatine to the right.

The best visit to the Roman Forum is the one made outside of it, following from high above an ideal itinerary that begins from Piazza Venezia. Along the Via dei Fori Imperiali (that starts from Piazza Venezia) we have on the right the *Basilica Emelia*. Burned and reconstructed many times in various epochs, it extends for about one hundred meters along four naves divided by marble columns. Some sculptured fragments of cornices and trabeations lying on the ground give an idea of the monumental dimensions and the decoration of Roman architecture in those particulars that today we consider minimal. We follow the Via Sacra towards the Capitol. At the limit of the Forum is the building of the *Curia*, the seat of the Roman Senate. Almost perfectly preserved even if without its external decoration, it has on the inside a sumptuous and intact floor inlaid with precious marbles of many colors. In front of the Curia there is an open area where political meetings were held for the election of public officials. Covered by a shed near this place, there is a little underground area in which

Temple of Vesta and another view of the Forum.

Below: Temple of Antoninus and Faustina.

we can see (under a slab of black marble, the famous *lapis niger*) a very ancient tomb of tufa, said to be that of Romulus. It bears the oldest known inscription in archaic Latin. Climbing back out we have in front of us the *triumphal arch of the Emperor Septimus Severus*, 23 meters high with three spans. It is almost completely covered with bas-reliefs and sculpture perfectly preserved.

To the left of the area (Still looking towards the Capitol) the real Forum extends, a vast square that during the Empire was paved with travertine and under which we can see part of the remains of the pavement of Republican times. Beyond the square there is the *Basilica Julia*, built on top of a primitive Republican edifice. It takes its name from the *Gens Julia*. Entirely covered with marble it had three naves divided by pilasters that are still partially visible. The remains of the portals and the streets that bounded it are also visible.

Above: House of the Vestals.

To the left of the Basilica Julia (looking at the Curia) rise eight monumental columns with trabeations. They are in an elevated position at the boundary of the forum. These columns are the remains of the portal of the *Temple of Saturn* in which the treasury was preserved. On the right there are three other monumental fluted columns, very elegant with their Corinthian capitals. They are the remains of the external portal of the *Temple of the Dioscuri*, raised on a high podium with stairs leading up to it. Nearby there are the remains of the *Temple of Julius Caesar*, erected by Augustus on the very spot where the body of Caesar was burned and where Anthony gave his famous

Below: Basilica
of Maxentius.

oration. Nearby we find the *Fonte di Giuturna*, a big covered basin dedicated to this god of the waters.

We proceed with our backs to the Capitol. Along the Via Sacra we see the rather devastated remains of the *Regia*, restored in later epochs. This was perhaps the residence of the kings and certainly that of the chief priests. In it was preserved, with the acts of the priests, the historical archives of the state. Near the Regia, fragments of a circular wall indicate the round building in which the eternal flame of Vesta was guarded. The conserving of this fire was one of the most ancient state liturgies, closely connected with the sacred origin of Rome. In the same building the most ancient relics were preserved, among which the famous *Palladio* that Aeneas brought from Troy, the oriental city that was the mythical ancestor-city of Rome. Nearby is the *Casa delle Vestali*, a rather well preserved building in which the rooms of the priestesses face a rectangular courtyard with a portal and cisterns.

Almost opposite the Regia on the other side of the Via Sacra there is a high stairway at the top of which rise the colossal columns of the *Temple of Antonino and Faustina*. The structure of this temple is almost completely intact because it later became a Christian church with the name of *San Lorenzo in Miranda*. Adjacent and also almost completely intact is the circular *Temple of the Divine Romulus* (the deified son of the Emperor Maxentius). This temple is decorated on the outside with columns of colored marble. The great bronze door is the original one and it functions perfectly. The other two bronze Roman doors are those of the

135

Curia and of the Baptistry of St. John, formerly in the Pantheon.

Following up-hill the Via Sacra, after the cemetery of which we have already spoken, we come to the *Basilica of Maxentius* that extends outside the limits of the forum and whose entrance is on Via dei Fori Imperiali. The edifice, begun by Maxentius between 306 and 312 A.D. and completed by Constantine, who modified its plan, constitutes in its remains one of the greatest architectural feats in the world for grandiosity, appearance, power, daring and rationality of construction. It was admired and studied by all of the artists of the Renaissance. Of it remain the three arched vaults with a central apse, of the right nave. It is incumbent on the center of Rome and on the forum itself. Symphonic concerts are held here on summer evenings.

Above: The Theater of Marcellus.

The Via Sacra, from whose last section we observe on the right some very interesting buildings of various periods, leads up to the hill called *Velia*, which is one of the three peaks of the Palatine (which see). At the center of the hill and like a crown for the road rises the *Arch of Titus*. Erected by the Senate to celebrate the victory over the Jewish people accomplished with the destruction of Jerusalem by Titus in 70 A.D., the arch has on the inside of its single span the depiction of the triumphal procession that brought to Rome the spoils from the Temple. (Easily visible is the seven-branched candlestick). We can also see the imperial chariot over which hangs Victory. At the center of the vault, in marble caissons, there is the apotheosis of Titus taken up to heaven by an eagle.

Forum Argentario

Exactly in the center of *Largo di Torre Argentina*, near Piazza Venezia and the Pantheon, at a level much lower than the present street, we see the remains of what for a certain period of ancient Roman history was the *Foro Argentario*, or the money changers' market. Here there are edifices of the Republican era in a fair state of preservation. Four temples placed beside each other rise in front of a square paved with travertine and flanked by portals under which the shops were lined up. These temples are interesting because they give an idea of what early Roman architecture was like. This made use of tufa more than the stone and marble of the imperial age. The third temple (coming from the direction of the Pantheon) is the oldest and even has Etruscan elements.

Below: a detail of Trajan's column.

Forum Olitorio

On *Via del Teatro di Marcello*, which takes its name from the edifice of the same name (which we see) and flanks the steepest side of the Capitol, there are three little temples. These make up part of what in antiquity was the *Foro Olitorio*, which would be our herb market. From the other side of the street part of the portal that surrounded it is visible, with its back to the Capitoline Hill. Some columns and some walls of the Republican era remain of the forum. Its plan cannot easily be reconstructed by the eye because of the construction afterwards of the little

137

church of *San Nicola in Carcere* on top of it, in the Christian era. In any case there were probably temples dedicated to *Giunione Sospita* (Juno the Liberator) and *Giano* (Janus).

Forum Boario

Still proceeding along Via del Teatro di Marcello (with our backs to Piazza Venezia, where the street begins) we see the temples of the zone of the *Foro Boario*, which would correspond to our modern cattle market. They are in a grassy open space slightly below the nearby *Lungotevere* and exactly opposite the church of Santa Maria in Cosmedin (which we see).

This is one of the oldest zones and is dedicated to Hercules, the mysterious god who in a certain sense stands behind the scenes of the official cult. His *Ara Massima* (high altar) must have been located at the *Area Sacra di Sant' Omobono* (under the present church of Sant'Omobono in front of the forum). This is near the *Arco di Giano Quadrifonte* (the Arch of the Four-faced Janus) between the Palatine and the Capitol. This is the spot on which it seems the foundation of Rome was prepared, the foundation later being attributed to Romulus. We find ourselves in what was called in ancient times the *Velabro*, or the swampy zone at the foot of the Palatine where the *Circus Maximus* (which we see) will later rise. This is also where legend says that the basket containing Romulus and Remus came to rest. The basket with Romulus and Remus in it had been thrown into the Tiber and was later found by an old shepherd. Then Ro-

Above: the tomb of the Emperor Augustus.

138

mulus and Remus were nourished by the she-wolf.

The two temples, modest in dimensions but perfect in their proportions, are very famous. The rectangular temple is of the type called *pseudo-periptero*. This means that it has a false external portal because instead of being detached from the main walls, its columns are attached to them. The construction is made of tufa, and it has Corinthian columns. It dates from the first century B.C. The name by which it is known throughout the world—*Tempio della Fortuna Virile*—is absolutely unauthentic. Its true name remains a mystery. The circular temple is of the period of the early empire and was probably restored in the III century A.D. It is bounded by twenty elegant, fluted Corinthian columns. (All except one are perfectly preserved). Also for this temple the famous name of *Tempio di Vesta* (Temple of Vesta) is not authentic. Mystery reigns over its true name and indeed over the entire zone. From here, going towards the church of Santa Maria in Cosmedin, we see the *Arch of the Four-faced Janus*. The large white rectangular structure made

Right: The Stadium of Domitian.

of travertine has four spans that open to the sides covered with niches at various heights. It has a fantastic and composite style typical of the last period of the Empire and hastily defined decadent. Next to this and of about the same period, with its back joined to the church of *San Giorgio in Velabro* (which we see), is the little *Arco degli Argentarii* with its rectangular span. It was dedicated by the money changers (argentarii) to the Emperor Septimus Severus and the Empress Julia Domna. We see here in addition to their portraits, that of their son Geta, killed by his brother Caracalla, who thus inherited the Empire. Caracalla condemned his victim to the *damnation memoriae* (a kind of official forbidding of recognition); because of this the portrait of Geta seems to have been accurately erased although it is still vaguely recognizable.

Above: a detail of the Via dei Fori Imperiali.

Imperial Forum

At the time of Julius Caesar, immediately before the beginning of the Empire, the Roman Forum no longer seemed sufficient for the handling of the public affairs of a city with a million inhabitants and on the way to becoming the ruler of a great part of Europe and the East. Therefore, Caesar erected a new forum that today is found to the left of the Altare della Patria at the beginning of Via dei Fori Imperiali (on the left side looking towards the Colosseum) at the foot of the Capitol. It is important because its elegant structures are the last of Republican archi-

Below: Arch of Constantine.

tecture. They will be followed by the much more imposing types of the imperial period. The *Tempio di Venere Genitrice* (Venus the Mother) rises in the center of a square bounded by portals under which we see well-preserved shops. Venus was considered the divine head of the Julian family.

Opposite this, on the other side of Via dei Fori Imperiali, still going towards the Colosseum, there begins one of the best-preserved and scenic monument zones of ancient Rome. At the old street level, much lower than the present one, and as if dominated by the two Baroque churches of *Santa Maria di Loreto* and of the *Nome di Maria* (that poetically integrate the whole) we see the *Foro Traiano* (Trajan's Forum), a great rectangular space (118×90 meters) paved with travertine and flanked by two portals. At the center there are the tall white columns of the *Basilica Ulpia*. Between this and the *Temple of Trajan* (situated under the two present churches) there were the famous Greek and Latin libraries, which haven't come down to us. Instead, the *Colonna Traiana* (Trajan's Column), which was originally between the libraries, has remained. The column was dedicated in 113 A.D. in celebration of the military enterprises of the emperor. 40 meters high and almost 4 meters in diameter, it is completely covered with a spiral band about one meter high, sculptured in low relief. Without a sense of continuity a succession of about 2500 figures unfolds on it, each one a complete work in itself. Only the *Colonna Antonina* (Antonine Column) is comparable to Trajan's Column. The Antonine Column was raised in 171 A.D. by the emperor Marcus Aurelius,

141

and it stands in Piazza Colonna near the monumental temple dedicated to *Neptune* by the Emperor Hadrian. Of this temple fifteen immense columns remain, now set into a wall.

As a crown to Trajan's Forum, with its back against the hill of the Quirinale, out of which a slope had to be cut, we find the *Mercati Traianei* (Trajan's Market) in a perfect state of preservation. There is a very large portal at the top of a few steps. It opens to a line of shops rationally structured. In front of it there is a portico of which remains numerous columns of precious marble.

The *Foro di Augusto* (Forum of Augustus) follows the Trajan Forum. It was erected by Augustus in the year 2 A.D. At its center rose the temple dedicated to *Marte Ultore* (Mars the Avenger, or better the « Justice-giver » or better still the « Regulator ». He was a god that Augustus wanted to honor after his victories over the enemies of Julius Caesar and his own permitted him to dedicate himself to the establishment and regulation of the Pax Romana (the Roman Peace). Only three fluted Corinthian columns of the surrounding portal remain of the temple, but these are sufficient to furnish with their beauty lessons in architecture to generations of artists. Raphael reproduced them in the scene of the *Burning of Borgo* in the Stanze Vaticane. Behind the temple is the immense wall erected to separate the zone from the workers' quarter called *Suburra*. The wall now joins the medieval façade of the early seat of the Knights of Malta. It has a beautiful balcony which overhangs the Trajan Markets.

Having left the Forum of Augustus and

Above: Trajan and Vittoriano's Forum.

Below: the pilasters
in the Baths of Caracalla.

crossed the modern Via Cavour, we see two columns topped by a trabeation with a statue of Minerva. These are all that remain of the *Foro di Nerva* (Nerva's Forum) or *Foro Transitorio*, near which rose the *Tempio della Pace* (the Temple of Peace).

The Via dei Fori Imperiali, before leading into the square in which the Colosseum rises, has on its right side the *Tempio di Venere e Roma* (of Venus and Rome), built in the II century A.D. by the Emperor Hadrian. It is a gigantic edifice in that style of Roman architecture comparable with the Baroque. Among the best examples which remain of it is Hadrian's Villa at Tivoli. The temple has two great cells with rhombus vaults lined on the same axis. We can say that they turn their backs to each other, uniting with the round apses. A portal, supported by a high podium and of which remain some of the immense 150 columns, surrounded it on all sides. Near the portal were the colossal statue (of Nero or the Sun?) that seems to have given its name to the Flavian Amphitheater (the Colosseum) and the fountain called *Meta Sudante.*

Going down the steps of this temple opposite the Colosseum and starting to the right of the wide Via dei Trionfi (along one of the sides of the Palatine) we see the *Arch of Constantine*, the last of the triumphal arches to be erected (315 A.D.). It is the most elaborate example of this type of monument, in which the plastic art reaches that perfection that a little later will be substituted by heavy barbarian forms. The figures of the barbarian soldiers that crown the eight external ornamental columns are of particular interest.

The Temple of Mars
in the Trajan Forum.

Fragments of
mosaics at the Baths
of Caracalla.

Colosseum and Imperial edifices

Proceeding along Via dei Trionfi, still along the side of the Palatine, we arrive at the place where the slopes of the hill form an angle, the valley of the *Circo Massimo* (Circus Maximus). It seems that this huge sports arena was begun at the end of the period of the kings, but we know for certain that it was built, originally in wood, at the end of the Republican period. It was principally designed to be a place for chariot races, of which the Romans were especially fond. During the Empire the palaces on the Palatine stood above it, and there was an enormous podium from which the court could attend the spectacles. Since the level of the street has raised since ancient times, the circus was buried—nearly intact—under a cover of earth that today would be very complicated and expensive to excavate, also because it would seem necessary to deviate an underground river. On today's street level we can see the ruins of only the higher tiers of seats, which have permitted making the zone into a hexagonal park, reproducing with vegetation the plan of the structures underground. The only way to understand its extent is to contemplate it from the Palatine. If at the end of Via dei Trionfi, instead of going toward the Circus Maximus, we turn to the left, following the tree lined *Passeggiata Archeologica* (archeological walk) we arrive at the present entrance to the *Terme di Caracalla* (Baths of Caracalla). The function of the baths for the ancient Romans is well known, at least for those who belonged to the lower social classes who, although all the houses had plumbing, couldn't afford the luxury of a private bath. The baths had three principal parts: *frigidarium, tepidarium,* and *calidarium,* but they also had gymnasiums equipped for physical education and also libraries, conference rooms, art galleries, and places to meet and to debate. Today nothing can suggest to us an idea of what the baths were at the highest point of Roman civilization. They were the everyday meeting place for the middle class. We can only say that in the Baths of Caracalla, in competition with those of Diocletian, there seems to have existed 1600 single baths in addition to the communal ones. To have an idea of their huge size it is enough to remember that in a small part of the inside it is possible to give a production of an opera like « Aida ». If we follow the edge of the Circus Maximus under the Palatine along the present *Via dei Cerchi* we return toward the Via del *Teatro di Marcello* in which the edifice of the same name rises. Begun by Caesar, it was completed by Augustus in 11 B.C. and dedicated to the memory of his nephew Marcello, the son of his sister Octavia, who had died some years before. It is wedged in among a complex of Renaissance and Baroque buildings that form a sort of wings (if we are looking from the Capitol). We can admire one side of it which is circular in form and which originally had three orders of arches (Doric, Jonic, and Corinthian starting from the bottom). The last of these orders was incorporated into the medieval structure of the fort of the Pierleoni, a baronial family which was

A general view
of the Via
dei Fori Imperiali.

A detail of the
Fori Imperiali.

succeeded by that of the Savelli (from which the zone takes the name of Monte Savello) and then by that of the Orsini. Under the Orsini the fortress assumed a very different character with the work—it seems—of Peruzzi. In any case the arches of the lower orders are perfectly preserved and are sometimes confused with those of the Colosseum by some tourists a bit distracted.

Now we return to the end of the Via dei Fori Imperiali in the zone in which the Colosseum rises. Looking at the monument (with our backs to Piazza Venezia) we have on our right the *Colle Oppio* (Oppian Hill). On the Colle Oppio and on the zone where we now find the Colosseum, the *Domus Aurea* (Golden House) once stood. It was the famous palace of Nero, built by actually drying up a pre-existing pond.

Very little remains of this labyrinthian structure because already in the Roman era it was knocked down to make room for the Colosseum (in the valley) and the *Terme di Tito* (Baths of Titus) and then the *Terme di Traiano* (Baths of Trajan) on the Colle Oppio. We have access to the ruins on the hill from the park of the same name on Via Labicana. These remains are half obliterated by all the restorations. They give just a little idea of their colossal grandiosity. It is colossal above all in the history of art and culture for its pictorial and sculptural decoration in the rooms. It is sufficient to say that in one of these rooms the groups of the Laocoon was found and that the term « grotesque painting » comes from these rooms reduced to grottoes when Raphael studied them.

The Colosseum, the most important monument of the zone, was begun by the

Three picturesque views
of the Colosseum seen
from the outside and inside.

Emperor Vespasian (of the Flavian family, from which its exact name of Flavian Amphitheater) in 72 A.D. and was completed by his son Titus in 80 A.D. It was designed to be a place for spectacles with gladiators and wild beasts. Its form is elliptic. The greater axis measures 188 meters, the smaller 156 meters. Its height is 57 meters. It stands on four floors that on the outside are composed of three levels, Doric, Ionic, and Corinthian respectively, and by a solid wall with Corinthian pilasters. The inside is composed, in the lower part, of boxes reserved for the court and the patricians, and in the upper part, of stone benches that come down like a funnel. Its capacity was about 50,000 spectators. A system of stairs, complicated but rigorous, admitted every spectator to his numbered seat. Under the floor of the arena there was (and the recent excavations have revealed its plan) a kind of fortress designed as the place for the cages of the wild animals, the gladiators, the facilities, and the real elevator that

brought men and animals from underground to the sight of the public. It seems—but the question is a controversial one—that a device, today unimaginable, which was built at the top of the highest tier and entrusted to squads of sailors, was able with a system of ropes and pulleys to extend a purple covering over the entire amphitheater when the burning sun bothered the Romans. The barbarians, the Barberini and other Roman families (that used its stones to construct their palaces), the earthquakes, ignorance, and the lack of care have reduced the Colosseum to what it is today. After Pius VII, who built the huge buttress to support it, many popes have taken it upon themselves to restore it.

In regard to historical vicissitudes, in the Middle Ages, the Colosseum served as a stone quarry; as a fortress in the struggles of the Roman baronial families, as a place of worhip when the practice of the Via Crucis (Way of the Cross) with the Lenten stations was instituted, and as a place of bad repute—especially at night. It was continually destroyed and restored and had the most unthinkable uses. The tradition according to which the Christians were martyred here is very doubtful if not to say impossible.

The Palatine

This is one of the Roman hills, on which the Roman emperors built their homes. According to legend, Romulus

Right: the beautiful bas-relief of *Augusto velato in corteo* (detail— Ara Pacis).

founded the primitive *città quadrata* (rectangular city) here in 753 B.C.

In the Middle Ages it was made into a fortress by the Frangipane family. Later the Farnese family transformed the upper part into gardens.

It is one of the most important archeological zones in the world.

ORTI FARNESIANI (Farnesian Gardens): These were built by the Farnese family. They are laid out on the top of the hill in the place where the Palace of Tiberius, enlarged by Trajan and Hadrian, originally stood. Of the Palace we can see a few ruins. In this vast Italian garden there is the *Casino* (little house) with a little temple sacred to the nymphs.

TEMPIO DI CIBELE (Temple of Cybele): Coming down from the Farnesian Gardens in the direction of the Circus Maximus in the so-called « Palatine area », we find the oldest archeological remains. Among these is the temple of the *Magna Mater* (Great Mother), or Cybele, which was erected in the II century B.C. and reconstructed by Augustus. In this zone there are also old constructions, ruins made of tufa, that are retained to belong to the house of Romulus, some steps of the stairway of Cacus, and remains of pre-historic huts.

CASA DI LIVIA (House of Lyvia): This is one of the best preserved buildings on the Palatine. It was thought to be the home of the wife of Augustus, but it now seems to be the one that the emperor had built for himself. It is the typical Roman *domus* with the rooms that look on to a central courtyard called the *peristilium*. On the

Above: the Domus Flavia.

Porta Appia or (Porta San Sebastiano).

right side there is the *triclinium* (the dining room) with its relative wine cellar. In front there are the three rooms of the *tablinum* with paintings in the Pompeian style.

CRIPTOPORTICO: To the left of the House of Lyvia we enter into the tunnel that runs along the side of the Palace of Tiberius. This underground passage is attributed to the epoch of Nero. Some examples of decoration in plaster remain of it.

PALAZZO DEI FLAVI (*Palace of the Flavians*): Climbing to the right from the underground passage we arrive at the Palace of the Flavians. It was built toward the end of the first century A.D. by Domitian. The *Domus Flavia* is situated on the top of the hill. It is composed of a type of portal behind which there are three parts. To the right there is the *Basilica* for the audiences given by the emperor. At the center there is the *Aula Regia* (residence). On the left there is the *Larario* or private chapel of the emperor. From the *Aula Regia* we go into the *peristilium* and the imperial *triclinium*. In these rooms there remain traces of paintings and mosaics of great interest.

DOMUS AUGUSTANA: This was also built by Domitian, and it was the private home of the emperors. It is a building that over-looks the Circus Maximus. It is built around a monumental courtyard and has several stories.

STADIO (*Stadium*): Situated near the Domus Augustana, this is an immense elliptical space with remains of constructions designed to be places for sports and spectacles. It is underneath the so-called imperial balcony, formed

The Arch of Giano.

The Arch of Titus.

by a great niche with a semi-circular dome.

TERME DI SETTIMIO SEVERO (Baths of Septimus Severus): To the east of the stadium we find the ruins of the Baths of Septimus Severus. These were supplied with water by the aqueduct of Claudius that began on Via Appia Antica, where there are some remains of it. Further south there are the constructions of Severus with the long terrace called the « belvedere ». From the terrace we admire a magnificent view that stretches from the Circus Maximus below to the Alban Hills.

Campidoglio

Two views of the Campidoglio.

The Campidoglio, or Monte Campidoglio, together with the Palatine (Palatino) is historically one of the most famous hills of Rome. Since its origin it has been one of the political and religious centers of the city. It is a steep hill that dominates the Roman Forum.

On the height where the Church of Aracoeli (Chiesa dell'Aracoeli) now stands the Temple of Juno (Tempio di Giunone) was located. Adjacent are the remains of the Temple of Jupiter Capitolinus (Tempio di Giove Capitolinus) and the Tabularium, on which the Senatorial Palace was built in the twelfth century.

In 1536 Michelangelo was commissioned to arrange the hill. The entrances to the Campidoglio are: the steep stairway that leads to the Church of the Aracoeli, the carriage ramp of Via delle Tre Pile, and the « Cordonata » (monumental staircase) that ascends gently and leads to the Plaza.

To one side of the Cordonata is the statue of Cola di Rienzo, who after having been elected tribune, was killed by the people in 1354. At the top of the Cordonata are two statues of Castor and Pollux, other ancient statues, trophies, and mile posts. In the center of the Square stands the statue of Marcus Aurelius. It is the only Roman equestrian statue that has remained whole through the centuries. The three palaces facing the Piazza Del Campidoglio are: The Senatorial Palace, today the City Hall of Rome, the Palace of the Conservatori, and the Palace of the Capitoline Museum (see Museums).

CARCERE MAMERTINO (*Mamertinus Prison*): Under the Church of San Giuseppe dei Falegnami (carpenters) by Giacomo Della Porta, is the Carcere Mamertino (its origins are uncertain and ascribed around 300 B.C.). Naw called the Chapel of San Pietro in Carcere, it consists of two chambers of which the upper is the true Carcere Mamertino. The lower chamber is a circular space called « Tullianum », and it was the State prison of ancient Rome. According to legend, Nero had Saint Peter imprisoned in it. In the lower chamber there is a small spring that Saint Peter is said to have spouted in order to baptize his two jailers, Processo and Martiniano, after having converted them.

Wall

The oldest Roman town walls are those attributed to Servius Tullius, one of the seven legendary kings; but it probably dates back to earlier times. Quite mon-

Below: Roman walls.

Above: Porta Pia and Porta San Sebastiano.

Below: Porta Pinciana.

umental are the remains of the walls that can be seen in the square of the central station (Termini) opposite the entrance shelter. However, the principal ancient walls are those by which, in around 260 A.D., the Emperor Aurelius closed the city for an extensive stretch, and are visible to some extent in numerous parts of the city today. The best preserved remains border the Corso d'Italia beginning at Via Veneto and extending monumentally, frequently fortified with towers, along the beginning of Via Appia, the area of San Giovanni and the pyramids of Caius Cestio.

Dating back to the IX century A.D. are the walls which Pope Leo IV ordered constructed to protect the primitive basilica of Saint Peter which had been looted by the Saraceni. Enlarged and restored by various Popes during the Renaissance these walls completely surround that which today is Vatican City. The most splendid part of the bastions can be admired from the zone of Piazza Risorgimento and from the entrances to the Vatican Museums.

The walls, begun in 1642 by Pope Urban VII, extend from Piazza di Porta Cavalleggeri up to the Gianicolo.

Doors

Among the most spectacular and best preserved doors remain the Appia (l'Appia), today called San Sebastiano, from which the Appian Way, the « regina viarum » (Queen of Roads) branched off. It is composed of a majestic arch bordered by two quite prominent semicircular embattled towers. From the inside, one can reach the top of the

Above: Porta San Paolo and Porta Latina.

Below: Porta Maggiore.

Aurelian walls which continue for a stretch of road and offer a beautiful view of the Roman countryside.

Inside the town-walls, in front of the Door of San Sebastiano there is a stately triumphal Roman arch, mistakenly called « di Druso ».

Since the age of the Emperors Onorio and Arcadio (IV century A.D.) who restored the present structure, stands the Porta Tiburtina (where the street of Via Tiburtina begins), today called the Porta San Lorenzo because of its proximity to the basilica. Its arch is also surrounded by two enormous crenelated towers on which stand the arches of the Marcio aqueduct, constructed by Augustus and restored by Tito and Caracalla.

Of exceptional artistic importance is the ancient Porta Praenestina, today called Porta Maggiore and from which the roads now called Casilina and Prenestina branch off. It is formed by a double row of majestic arches laid upon the aqueduct of Claudio. Close to it, outside the town walls is the unmistakable funerary monument of the baker Eurisace (supplier of the state during the republican era) constructed to give the impression of an oven for bread baking.

Of the Roman era and spectacularly embellished with towers and battlements (following the road along the Mura Aureliane) are Porta Metronia and Porta Latina. However they do not attain the picturesque effect of Porta Ostiense, today called Porta San Paolo, because of its proximity to the basilica of that name. Its construction is formed of two arches on the inside portion and one arch on the outside; caused

155

by the difference in date of construction of the two high bordering towers. This door is close to the famous Pyramid of Caio Cestio (Piramide di Caio Cestio), funerary monument erected in 43 B.C. (base is 30 meters, height 37 meters) of white travertine. Behind the pyramid is found the cosy and romantic garden of the Protestant cemetery or Cimitero degli Inglesi, in which the remains of the poets Keats and Shelley and the son of Goethe are buried.

Porta del Popolo known as the « official » door to Rome was used by pilgrims and persons of renown dating back to the Anni Santi (Holy Years). The door rises on the same site as the ancient Porta Flaminia (which street of the same name led to the north). The external crenelated façade is attributed to Vignola (1561) probably taken from a design of Michelangelo. The internal façade was decorated by Bernini in 1655. This famous door claims the entry of Carlo VIII of France (1494) and Christina of Sweden (the only woman buried in Saint Peter's) in 1655. The internal façade (which leads to the Via Nomentana) is also a Michelangelo design. On September 20, 1870, a few meters from the Porta del Popolo the « breach » through which the troops of the Italian Kingdom entered Rome to conquer it and to make it the Italian capital, was opened in the Aurelian walls.

Among the numerous historical and artistic doors which enrich Rome, one cannot forget to mention San Pancrazio. Rebuilt by Vespignani in the XIX

View along the Tiber.

Porta del Popolo.

century on a pre-existent base of the Temple of Urbano VIII, it crowns the top of the Gianicolo, a zone rich in memories of battles during the Italian Risorgimento. Not to be forgotten is the baroque Porta Portese located in Trastevere near the ancient Porto di Ripa Grande, on the Tiber. The well known and characteristic market of antiques and old wares of all kinds, takes place here every Sunday morning.

Historical Monuments

CASTEL SANT'ANGELO (or *Mausoleum of Hadrian*): The form is a circular tower built on a square foundation. It was begun by Emperor Hadrian and terminated by his successor Antonius Pius. The remains of the Emperors Hadrian to Settimo Severo and their families were placed here. Subsequently, under the name of Castel Sant'Angelo the building became a fortress, residence of princes and popes, and was later turned into a prison and military barracks.

Castel Sant'Angelo reflects the historical events of Rome. The four lateral towers constructed by Sangallo under Pope Alexander VI were added later. Of the primitive Roman construction only the central cylindrical mass of travertine marble blocks remains. It is crowned by the Loggia of Pope Julius II. The top tower, crowned with Bernini's statue « Angel with the Sword »,

Castel Sant'Angelo:
a general view and
a view of the Tiber.

157

was once the foundation of the Imperial statue. In front of the castle one finds the Bridge of Sant'Angelo dating back to the Roman era. It is decorated with statues of the Apostles Peter and Paul and other statues of angels, from the school of Bernini.

MAUSOLEUM OF AUGUSTUS (Mausoleo di Augusto): Constructed (27 B.C.) by Emperor Augustus as a sepulchre for himself and his family. A circular structure decorated with marbles and statues, bordered by porticoes and crowned by a conical mound of earth on which there was a statue of the Emperor.

ARA PACIS AUGUSTAE: It was erected in 13 B.C. in honour of the Emperor Augustus to celebrate the long peace he gave Rome. In 1938 it was reconstructed almost completely with the original fragments but not on its original site. The Ara is enclosed by a marble wall decorated on both sides with bas reliefs which illustrate the life and works of the Emperor.

THE ALTAR OF THE NATION (L'Altare della Patria): Dedicated to Victor Emanuel II, first King of Italy. It was begun in 1885 and finished in 1911. A portico of sixteen columns flanked by propylae dominates the complex. On the propylae, of eight columns each are two bronze quadrigae. A stairway decorated by allegorical statues leads to the Altar of the Nation. It is crowned by the statue of Rome at the foot of which the Tomb of the Unknown Soldier holds the mortal remains of an unknown Italian soldier who perished in the first World War.

Above: the Palazzo del Quirinale.

158

Below: Palazzo della Consulta.

PORTICO D'OTTAVIA: The remains of this portico consist of a monumental entrance of Corinthian columns, which is part of a magnificent building constructed by Ottavia, sister of Emperor Augustus. They were saved from total destruction by Pope Stephen III, who in 770 joined to them the small church of Sant'Angelo in Pescheria (thus named because it was the site of the fish market during the Middle Ages). The floor was restored in 203 following a fire, by the Emperors Settimio Severo and Caracalla. The structure was composed of two rows of eight Corinthian columns of which there remain two outside and three inside. To the right and left were two rows of fourteen columns; the longer sides consisted of forty or more columns. The arcade must have contained about three hundred columns completely surrounding the two temples of Jupiter and Juno (not to be confused with those found on the Capitoline hill). A medieval arch later replaced two fallen columns near the façade of the Church. The arcade rises near the Tiber (Tevere) practically in front of the Island of Tiberina.

SYNAGOGUE (*Sinagoga*): It is the temple of the Jewish Community of Rome. Constructed in 1904 in a vaguely Syro-Babylonian style. Its vast dome with a quadrangular base of aluminum is visible from the heights of the city. It is located on the outskirts of the district, which in the XVI century gave rise to the « ghetto », a section in which the Jews were confined and subject to discriminatory and oppressive actions. The gates of the ghetto were demolished when Rome became the capital of Italy in 1870.

159

Palaces

PALAZZO DEL QUIRINALE: Erected on one of the highest hills of Rome; built as a summer residence for Popes, it was begun by Gregory XIII. Ceremonies and conclaves were held in the palace and the names of the Popes were announced and solemn blessings were given from the lodge that beautifies the façade. The building was begun by Flaminio Ponzio and Mascheroni, continued by Domenico Fontana, Carlo Maderno, Bernini, and was completed by Fuga. An ancient fortified glacis leans on the left of the façade. The main doorway is the work of Bernini. In the interior, a sumptuous stairway, dominated by a fresco of Melozzo da Forlì, « Christ in Glory among the Angels » leads to a marvelous and vast courtyard. The most interesting rooms are the Salone dei Corazzieri, la Cappella Paolina, Cappella dell'Annunciata with the « Annunciation » by Guido Reni. The gardens are magnificent. After 1870 the palace became the residence of the Kings of Italy. It has been the official residence of the Italian Republic's President since 1946.

PALAZZO DELLA CONSULTA: Also in the square of the Quirinale is the Palace of the Council (Palazzo della Consulta) with its eighteenth century façade designed by Fuga. From the inside courtyard one sees the spectacular stairway. Next to it is the monumental Pallavicini-Rospigliosi palace built by Vasari and Maderno on the remains of Constantine's palace. In the courtyard of the palace is the Rospigliosi Casino with the famous fresco of « Aurora » by Guido Reni.

Palazzo Farnese.

The facade of Palazzo Corsini.

Palazzo Venezia.

Palazzo della
Cancelleria.

PALAZZO VENEZIA: Built between 1455 and 1464 for the Cardinal Pietro Barbo, who later became Pope Paul II, from the plans attributed to Leon Battista Alberti. The manificent portico of the courtyard is the work of Giuliano da Maiano. Several popes lived in the palace. It was donated to the Republic of Venice (from which it took its name) by Pius IV and in 1797 it was the seat of the Austro-Hungarian Embassy of the Vatican. In 1916 it was given to the Italian government.

The palace was the official seat of government during Fascism. Now it is the seat of art and historical collections.

PALAZZO BRASCHI: Built at the end of the eighteenth century for the nephews of Pope Pius VII, Braschi. On one of the external walls of the Palace leans the famous statue of Pasquino, a mutilated torso of the Classic Age, on whose pedestal the Romans applied their political satire with inscriptions. The Palace is now the seat of the Museum of Rome.

PALAZZO FARNESE: Presently the seat of the French Embassy, its construction was begun in 1514 for the Cardinal Alessandro Farnese, later Pope Paul III, by Antonio da Sangallo the younger. Michelangelo added the large windows and the frame with Farnesian lilies. Giacomo Della Porta finished it. In the courtyard of the « three orders » the second is the work of Michelangelo. There are two sarcophagi, one comes from the Baths of Caracalla (Terme di Caracalla), and the other, according to legend, contains the ashes of Cecilia Metella, which come from the great tomb of Metella on the Via Appia. The beautiful sixteenth century palace is also famous for the decoration with frescoes of mythological subjects on the vault and on the walls of the large gallery on the first floor. These are the works of Annibale Carracci.

PALAZZO DELLA CANCELLERIA: It is one of the most valuable fifteenth century buildings in Rome. It was built for the nephew of Pope Sisto IV, Cardinal Raffaele Riario. The name of the architect is not certain but the style of the long façade with the arched windows decorated with pilasters suggest the work of Andrea Bregno. The courtyard, with two lines of arcades with columns, shows the Bramante architectural style. In the salon on the first floor the frescoes by Vasari illustrate the life of Paul III. The palace is the seat of the Pontifical Chancellor.

PALAZZO MONTECITORIO: It is the seat of the Chamber of Deputies (Chamber of Commons). It was begun by Bernini in 1650 and finished by Carlo Fontana in 1690.

Above: Palazzo di Montecitorio.

PALAZZO CHIGI: It is the seat of the President of the Council of Ministers. Begun in 1562 by Giacomo Della Porta, continued by Carlo Maderno and brought to completion by Felice Della Greca.

PALAZZO MADAMA: Seat of the Italian Senate since 1871. Built in the sixteenth century for the Medici family and named after Madame Margherita of Austria, the wife of Alessandro de' Medici. The baroque façade is the work of Cardi and of Marucelli.

PALAZZO DI VILLA MEDICI: Seat of the French Academy; built in 1544

162

by Annibale Lippi for Cardinal Ricci of Montepulciano. It later became the property of the Grand Dukes of Tuscany, taking the name of Villa Medici. In 1803 Napoleon transferred the Academy of Fine Arts, formed by Colbert under Louis XIV.

PALAZZO CORSINI: Constructed in baroque style by Ferdinando Fuga in 1732. Noteworthy are the vestibule and grand stairway. It is the seat of the Academy of the Lincei.

PALAZZO DELLA FARNESINA: Called Villa Farnesina, built by Baldassare Peruzzi for the Sienese banker Agostino Chigi, transferred to the Farnese family then to the Borbons of Naples and finally to the Italian government. On the ground floor the « Banchetto degli Dei » (Banquet of the Gods) and « Scene della favola di Amore e Psiche» (Scenes from the story of Cupid and Psyche) can be found. They were painted by Raphael and his pupils. In the Galatea Salon is Raphael's fresco « Galatea che sfugge l'amore di Polifemo » (Galatea fleeing from the love of Polyphemus). On the first floor is the Salon of the « Prospettive » by Peruzzi and the room in which Sodoma painted the « Nozze di Alessandro e Rossana » (the Wedding of Alexander and Roxane).

PALAZZO BARBERINI: Begun in 1625 by Maderno and Borromini, it was completed by Bernini to whom the façade, in three orders, is attributed. Pietro da Cortona also participated in these works and painted the fresco on the vault of the *salone* which bears his name.

Below: Museum of Villa Borghese.

Museums

THE NATIONAL MUSEUM (*Museo Nazionale Romano*): This museum is also called Museo delle Terme. Collected here are works of Greek, Roman, and Christian art. In several halls of the Terme (baths) are well preserved various examples of mosaic pavements, sarcophaghi, and the reconstruction of the Tetrestyle Temple of Terranuova (II Century).

MUSEUM OF PALAZZO VENEZIA (*Museo di Palazzo Venezia*): It is located in the Palace bearing the same name and occupies the rooms of the apartment of Barbo (Paul II) and the apartment of Cybo (Innocent VIII). There are collections of pictures and paintings, terracotta reliefs, fragments of frescoes, furniture, tapestries, porcelain, small bronze collections and an armoury.

THE CAPITOLINE MUSEUM (*Museo Capitolino*): Located in the Capitoline Palace (Palazzo Capitolino), it has the most ancient collection of sculptures of the Classical age, established by Sistus IV in the XV century. Several Popes have enriched the museum with additional art works.

MUSEUM OF THE CONSERVATORI (*Museo dei Conservatori*): Located in the Palace of the Conservatori in the Campidoglio square. It also includes the New Museum (Museo Nuovo) and the Pinacoteca Capitolina.

MUSEUM OF ROME (*Museo di Roma*): It is located in the Palazzo Bras-

Above: a view of the facade of Palazzo Barberini.

Below: detail
of the pediment of the
Portico di Ottavia.

chi and it gathers evidence of customs of Rome from the Middle Ages to present time, in an historicaltopografic documentation.

MUSEUM OF CASTEL SANT'ANGELO: There are collections of objects concerning the various historical periods of the castle. It also includes the Historical Military Museum (Museo Storico Militare).

THE DORIA PAMPHILI GALLERY (Galleria Doria Pamphili): It is located on the first floor of the homonymous palace, erected in the fifteenth century. The eighteenth century façade in rococo style is the work of Valvassorri. The Gallery includes some Italian and foreign masterpieces from the XVI to the XVII century (Valasquez, Raphael, Caravaggio, Titian, Correggio, Tintoretto, Parmigianino, Poussin, Rubens, etc.).

NATIONAL GALLERY OF MODERN ART (Galleria Nazionale d'Arte Moderna): Located in the Valle Giulia near the Villa Borghese, it is the most important collection of works by Italian sculptors and painters of the nineteenth and twentieth centuries. These works represent all the currents of painting of this period.

BORGHESE GALLERY (Galleria Borghese). It is located in the famous homonymous villa and the works of the greatest artists are collected here: Titian, Raphael, Botticelli, Andrea del Sarto, Lorenzo di Credi, Domenichino, Caravaggio, etoc., and sculptures of Lisippo, Canova, Bernini, etc.

NATIONAL GALLERY OF ANCIENT ART (Galleria Nazionale di Arte Antica) (Barberini Palace): Here are gath-

One of the most beautiful rooms in the Borghese Gallery.

ered pre-existent collections among which are those from Palazzo Corsini, and the Torlonia. There are works of many famous masters: Van Dyck, Rubens, Murillo, Guido Reni, Guercino, Dolci, Baciccia, Perugino, Raphael, etc.

ACADEMY OF SAINT LUKE (Accademia di San Luca): It is the oldest academy of Fine Arts in the world and it includes a gallery of painting and works by Titian, Baciccia, Bronzino, etc., and a fragment of a fresco by Raphael.

MUSEUM OF ROMAN CIVILIZATION (Museo della Civiltà Romana). It rises in the new residential area of the EUR and presents a complete and documented review of the history, religion, costume, and ancient institutions of Rome, with numerous archeological reproductions and exhibits, and plastic art and moulds built in scale, which are of great interest.

Bridges

Among the best preserved ancient Roman briges are, without doubt, the two that join the Island Tiberina (L'Isola Tiberina) to the mainland, the Cestio (on the side of Trastevere), and the Fabricio (near the center of the city). In reality they are aligned to form one bridge which extends to the left and right of the river-island.

Erected in 62 B.C., the Cestio was restored in 1892; both bridges carry interesting inscriptions of emperors and officials. The Fabricio is also called Ponte Quattro Capi, and has ancient

Above: the beautiful Roman bridge of Nona, on the Via Prenestina and a view of the island Tiberina.

Below: Perspective view of Ponte Vittorio, Ponte S. Angelo and Ponte Umberto I.

sculptures of a four-spring fountain (that were placed there when the name was already in use). The origin of the island is unknown. It rises at the center of the widest part of the river. Its primitive history, according to legend, is connected with the expulsion of the Tarquinii Kings. It is shaped exactly as a ship and the Romans, enclosing the bridge's stone borders, decorated it as the keel of a ship. It became sacred during the worship· of Esculapius, Greek God of Medicine. A large sanctuary-hospital was built and on those remains the Church of San Bartolomeo all'Isola was erected during the Christian era. Opposite this church (on the island) stands the Ospedale dei Fatebenefratelli, a Renaissance structure.

Another most renowned bridge of the Roman age is the Ponte Milvio (until a few years ago called Ponte Molle). Nearby, in the year 312, Constantine conquered Massentius. This victory marked the permanent affirmation of Christian faith. Tradition says that before the battle, Constantine had a vision of a cross on which was written, « In hoc signo vinces », « You will win with this sign ». At the bridge's outlet, going out of the city, one sees the massive tower of Valadier.

Of particular interest are the so-called Ponte Rotto (Broken Bridge) consisting of a few stately arches which remained standing after the collapse in 1598, of what had been the reconstruction of the ancient Ponte Emilio, ordered by Pope Paul V; and the Ponte Nomentano that passes onver the Aniene River along the Via Nomentana. It is decorated with towers and embattlements, against a background of a verdant hill.

Ponte Milvio.

Piazza Colonna.

(It is said that in the surroundings Pope Leo III solomnly received the German Emperor Charlemagne who came to Rome for the coronation in the ninth-century).

Restructured during the last century, the Sisto Bridge (of the Renaissance) (Ponte Sisto), leads from the center of the city to the heart of Trastevere, coming out in front of the monumental fountain placed at the foot of the Gianicolo hill. It is dominated from above by the fountain of San Pietro in Montorio.

Among the numerous modern bridges we shall name only, Ponte Cavour (opposite the XIX century Palace of Justice), Ponte Margherita and Ponte Matteotti (near Piazzale Flaminio), Ponte Umberto (near Corso Umberto in the direction of Saint Peter's), Ponte Risorgimento (approximately between the hills of Parioli and Monte Mario), and Ponte Mazzini (opposite Trastevere) in construction for a subway (metropolitana).

Squares

PIAZZA DEL QUIRINALE: In the center of it stands the obelisk with the fountain and the statue of the Dioscuri, « Castor » and « Pollux ». They are Roman replicas from the original Greek works of the IV and V centuries B.C.

PIAZZA NAVONA: It preserves the shape and dimensions of the Stadium of Domitian, on which it was built. The baroque style is predominant here. In the center of the square is the

Fountain of Rivers, by Bernini; dominated by an obelisk. The great statues represent the Nile, the Ganges, the Danube and the Rio della Plata. The Fountain of the Moon, also designed by Bernini, and the other more modern one of Neptune are at the extremes of the Piazza.

PIAZZA DI SPAGNA: Its name is derived from the homonymous palace, seat of the Spanish Embassy to the Holy See since the XVII century. In front of the palace is the memorial column of the « Immaculate Conception » erected in 1856 by Pius IX. A spectacular stairway, the work of De Sanctis and Specchi, leads to the Church of Trinità dei Monti. At the foot of the stairway is the fountain named « Barcaccia », work of Pietro Bernini, father of Lorenzo.

PIAZZA DELLA REPUBBLICA: Commonly called Piazza Esedra, built in 1885, it is limited by two porticoes that follow the perimeter of the central exedra of the Baths of Diocletian (Terme di Diocleziano). In the center is the Fountain of the Naiads by Guerrieri, with groups of bronzes by Rutelli. The façade of Santa Maria degli Angeli opens onto the Piazza.

PIAZZA DEL POPOLO: It was designed at the beginning of the XIX century by Valadier, who spectacularly planned, with slopes and fountains, the dominating hill of the Pincio. In the center of the square stands the Egyptian Obelisk from the time of Ramesse II, transferred here by order of Sistus V, from the Circus Maximus xhere it had been placed by Augustus. On the

Piazza Venezia.

Piazza del Popolo.

A picturesque view
of the stairway of
Trinità dei Monti.

opposite side of the Pincio slopes, under the double exedra, are the two fountains formed by the groups « Rome between the Tiber » and the « Aniene and Neptune with the Tritons ». Access to Via Flaminia is through the Renaissance Porta dei Popoli, contiguous to the Church of Santa Maria del Popolo (see Churches).

Opposite the door, the square is closed in by two symmetrically placed baroque churches, Santa Maria dei Miracoli and Santa Maria in Montesanto (begun by Rainaldi and completed by Bernini and Fontana).

PIAZZA TRINITÀ DEI MONTI: The stairway that leaves Piazza di Spagna (see) leads to Piazza Trinità dei Monti, on which the façade of the church of the same name, opens; (see). This square, small and with an obelisk at its center, is important mainly for its view: at it foot are the sections that surround Castel Sant'Angelo and Saint Peter's, rising in the background. To the left is the opening of the Via Gregoriana and Sistina, with a view of baroque palaces. To the right the vast and long tree-lined panoramic walk dominating the famous Via Margutta, and a series of roof-gardens and terraces (mostly homes and studios of artists, leads to the Pincio, see).

PIAZZA DELL'ESQUILINO: It is the site where the monumental and spectacular baroque apse of Santa Maria Maggiore rises, at the top of the ancient Esquilino hill. In front of the large and graceful stairway that sustains this apse rises an obelisk.

LARGO DELLE QUATTRO FONTA-NE: It is so called because at the four corners of this big cross-road there are as many fountains (placed in the baroque age) and statues and ancient fragments. Its peculiarity is derived from its position. At a distance one can see the obelisks of Trinità dei Monti, of Piazza del Quirinale and of the Esquilino (see). Ascending from Piazza Barberini one faces the façade of San Carlino alle Quattro Fontane with its adjoining convent. Both are works of Borromini.

PIAZZA DELLA ROTONDA: This the Pantheon and its name « della Rotonda » is simply due to the fact that the Pantheon is round.
Facing the temple: at the left is the Hotel of the Sun (Albergo del Sole), preferred by Ludovico Ariosto during his Roman sojourns four centuries ago. It has remained almost completely intact since that era; at the right one faces the posterior part of the monumental Palazzo Giustiniani, a masterpiece of the Renaissance. It was completed by Barocco. In the center of the square is a small Egyptian obelisk.

A general view of
Piazza Navona and
a detail of the
Fontana dei Quattro Fiumi.

PIAZZA DELLA MINERVA: Still facing the façade of the Pantheon, one finds at a short distance, the façade of Santa Maria sopra Minerva (see Churches). The importance of this small piazza is attributed to an odd statue. The astute tourist will see ancient Egyptian civilization unified with that of the Renaissance. The monument is an Egyptian obelisk resting on the back of a statue of an elephant (end of XVI century). To one side of the pedestal sustaining the elephant a stone tablet, inscribed in Latin, states that Egyptian knowledge can be assimilated and endured only by he who posseses an intelligence equal to the strength of an elephant. Not by chance, the monument rises on a site (near the Pantheon) dedicated to the God of Wisdom.

Fountains

FOUNTAIN OF TREVI (*Fontana di Trevi*): It is the most monumental fountain in Rome. Nicola Salvi began its construction in 1733 on order from Clement XII. The fountain was finished in 1762. It is formed of fountains, rocks and grottoes decorated with statues. In the central niche is the famous Neptune drawn by marine horses and tritons. In the two lateral niches we find: to the right, the Operosita, and to the left, the Abbondanza.

FOUNTAIN OF TRITON (*Fontana del Tritone*): Attributed to Bernini (1673), it is in the center of Piazza Barberini.

FOUNTAIN OF THE TURTLES (*Fontana delle Tartarughe*): A jewel of the Renaissance, it is formed by four extremely elegant bronze youngsters playing with turtles.

FOUNTAIN OF SAN PIETRO IN MONTORIO (*Fontana di San Pietro in Montorio*): Located on the Gianicolo, giving a panoramic view of the city. It was built by Domenico Fontana and Carlo Maderno (in 1612) by order of Paul V.

Above:
a general view
of the famous
Fontana di Trevi.

Villas

VILLA BORGHESE: One of the largest public parks created for Cardinal Scipione Borghese at the beginning of the XVII century, it was bought by the Italian government and donated to the City. Among magnificent paths, numerous fountains and statues, pine-woods and squares surrounded by old trees, stands the Casino Borghese. Built by Vasanzio as a summer residence for Cardinal Scipione Borghese, it is the seat of the Borghese Gallery of Art (see Galleries).

PINCIO: It is the garden located on the homonymous hill. It was designed by Valadier in the neo-classical style. The terrace of the large square which overlooks Piazza del Popolo offers one of the best views of Rome: to the right, Monte Mario; to the front, the Dome of Saint Peter's; in the background, the Gianicolo hill; to the left, the Quirinal and the Vittoriano.

Below: left, the Fontana del Tritone; right, the Fontana delle Tartarughe.

VILLA PAMPHILI: It is the largest park in Rome having a perimeter of more than nine kilometers. The Algardi Casino (1650) is located in a setting of groves, lawns, lakes, Italian-style gardens, and motifs of English parks. It has recently been opened to the public.

VILLA CELIMONTANA: Its position is particularly picturesque because it is located in a spacious and airy zone at the top of the Celio. It has many rare and exotic plants and antique objects. It also has a beautiful panoramic terrace.

175

VILLA ADA: It is located on the Salaria and has a luxuriant park. Former residence of the Italian royal family, it is at present opened to the public.

VILLA SCIARRA: Multicolored peacocks walk among the shady and silent paths of this Villa, and for this reason some call it « the Villa of the peacocks ».

GIANICOLO: It is the only one of the historical hills of Rome that rises on the left bank of the Tiber and has been consecrated since the beginning of the city's history to the worship of Gianus (Giano), hence the name of the hill. Because of the difficult identification of Gianus in Roman liturgy, the past events of the hill have remained quite mysterious.

On the contrary, its modern history is well known. In 1849 with the cannonade and the destruction of the « Villa Medici del Vascello » the destiny of the Roman Republic, with, above all, the work of Giuseppe Mazzini, succeeded in replacing the supremacy of the Popes during the first rebellions of the Italian Risorgimento. It succeeded for a short time.

There are many slopes and roads that climb to the Gianicolo, a lengthy hill that dominates the Trastevere section. Its summit is crowned by a tree-lined avenue at the center of which is a large square (piazzale) (decorated with the statue of Giuseppe Garibaldi) from which it is possible to gaze upon Rome.

Detail of a fresco in the Sistina Chapel: the *Creator*.

SOUVENIRS
OF THE JUBILEE

AUTOGRAPHS

ROMAN ADDRESSES

MEMORANDUM

ITINERARIES

1st ITINERARY: Porta San Sebastiano – Catacomba di San Callisto – Catacomba di San Sebastiano – Catacomba di Domitilla – Via Appia Antica – Tomba di Cecilia Metella.

2nd ITINERARY: Santa Cecilia in Trastevere – S. Crisogono – Santa Maria in Trastevere – Palazzo Corsini – Palazzo della Farnesina – Sant'Onofrio – Gianicolo – San Pietro in Montorio – Villa Sciarra – Catacombe di S. Pancrazio e Chiesa – Villa Pamphili.

3rd ITINERARY: S. Sisto Vecchio – Terme di Caracalla – Santi Nereo e Achilleo – S. Gregorio Magno – Santi Quattro Coronati – S. Maria in Domnica – Villa Celimontana – S. Martino ai Monti – SS. Giovanni e Paolo – Santo Stefano Rotondo – S. Giovanni a Porta Latina.

4th ITINERARY: San Pietro in Vincoli – Piazza dell'Esquilino – Santa Maria Maggiore – Santa Pudenziana – Santa Prassede – SS. Marcellino e Pietro – S. Clemente – S. Giovanni in Laterano – Battistero di San Giovanni – La Scala Santa – Santa Croce in Gerusalemme – San Lorenzo Fuori le Mura.

5th ITINERARY: Museo di Villa Giulia – Villa Borghese – Galleria Borghese – Pincio – Villa Medici – Chiesa e Piazza Trinità dei Monti – Scalinata di Trinità dei Monti e Piazza di Spagna – Accademia di San Luca – Fontana del Tritone – S. Maria della Concezione (detta I Cappuccini) – Palazzo Barberini – Galleria Nazionale.

6th ITINERARY: Piazza del Quirinale – Palazzo del Quirinale – Palazzo della Consulta – Sant'Andrea al Quirinale – Largo Quattro Fontane – Santa Susanna – Porta Pia – Santa Costanza – Catacomba e Chiesa di Sant'Agnese – Catacombe di Priscilla – Villa Ada.

7th ITINERARY: Piazza San Pietro – Basilica di San Pietro – Grotte Vaticane – Museums and Galleries of the Vatican City.

8th ITINERARY: Pantheon – Piazza della Rotonda – Santa Maria Sopra Minerva – Piazza della Minerva – Sant'Ignazio di Loyola – San Luigi dei Francesi – Sant'Agostino – Santa Maria dell'Anima – Santa Maria della Pace – Piazza Navona – Palazzo Madama – Sant'Agnese in Agone.

9th ITINERARY: Chiesa del Gesù – Sant'Andrea della Valle – Palazzo Braschi e Museo di Roma – Palazzo della Cancelleria – San Lorenzo in Damaso – Chiesa Nuova o Santa Maria in Vallicella – Castel Sant'Angelo – Museo di Castel Sant'Angelo.

10th ITINERARY: Foro Boario – Foro Argentario – Fontana delle Tartarughe – Sinagoga – Portico di Ottavia – San Bartolomeo all'Isola – San Giorgio in Velabro – Santa Maria in Cosmedin – Santa Anastasia – Santa Sabina – Santa Prisca – San Saba – Basilica di San Paolo Fuori le Mura – Museo della Civiltà – San Paolo alle tre fontane.

11th ITINERARY: Campidoglio – Museo Capitolino – Museo dei Conservatori – Santa Maria d'Aracoeli – Altare della Patria – San Marco – Palazzo Venezia – Museo di Palazzo Venezia.

12th ITINERARY: Foro Romano – Carcere Mamertino – SS. Luca e Martina – Santa Maria Antiqua – SS. Cosma e Damiano – Santa Francesca Romana.

13th ITINERARY: Palatino – Colosseo ed Edifici Imperiali – Fori Imperiali.

14th ITINERARY: Piazza della Repubblica – Santa Maria degli Angeli – Museo Nazionale Romano – San Vitale – Basilica dei Santi Apostoli – Museo Doria Pamphili – San Marcello – Palazzo Chigi – Palazzo Montecitorio – Fontana di Trevi – San Silvestro in Capite – San Carlo al Corso – Mausoleo di Augusto – Ara Pacis.

ADDRESSES

BASILICAS AND CHURCHES
AND CHURCHES

Basilica di San Pietro: Piazza San Pietro.
Basilica di Santa Maria Maggiore: Piazza Santa Maria Maggiore.
Basilica di San Giovanni in Laterano: Piazza San Giovanni in Laterano.
Basilica di San Paolo fuori le Mura: Via Ostiense.

S. Agnese in Agone: Piazza Navona.
S. Agostino: Piazza S. Agostino.
S. Anastasia: Piazza S. Anastasia.
S. Andrea al Quirinale: Via del Quirinale, 29.
S. Andrea della Valle: Piazza Vidoni, 6.
SS. Apostoli: Piazza SS. Apostoli, 51.
S. Bartolomeo all'Isola: Via Isola Tiberina, 22.
S. Carlo al Corso: Via del Corso, 437.
S. Cecilia: Piazza S. Cecilia, 22.
S. Clemente: Via Labicana, 95.
SS. Cosma e Damiano: Via dei Fori Imperiali, 1.
S. Costanza: Via Nomentana, 349.
S. Crisogono: Piazza Sonnino, 4.
S. Croce in Gerusalemme: Piazza S. Croce in Gerusalemme.
S. Francesca Romana: Piazza S. Francesca Romana.
Gesù: Piazza del Gesù.
S. Giorgio in Velabro: Via del Velabro, 19.
S. Giovanni a Porta Latina: Via di Porta Latina, 17.
SS. Giovanni e Paolo: Piazza SS. Giovanni e Paolo, 13.
S. Gregorio: Via S. Gregorio, 1.
S. Ignazio di Loyola: Piazza S. Ignazio.
S. Lorenzo in Damaso: Piazza della Cancelleria, 1.
S. Lorenzo fuori le Mura: Piazzale del Verano, 3.
SS. Luca e Martina: Via della Curia, 8.
S. Luigi dei Francesi: Piazza S. Luigi dei Francesi, 5.
SS. Marcellino e Piero: Via Merulana, 162.
S. Marcello: Piazza S. Marcello, 5.
S. Marco: Piazza S. Marco, 8.
S. Maria Antiqua: Foro Romano.
S. Maria d'Ara Coeli: Scala dell'Arce Capitolina, 18.
S. Maria degli Angeli: Piazza della Repubblica.
S. Maria dell'Anima: Via della Pace, 20.
S. Maria della Concezione (detta I Cappuccini): Piazza dei Cappuccini (angolo Via Veneto).

S. Maria della Pace: Via della Pace, 5.
S. Maria del Popolo: Piazza del Popolo, 12.
S. Maria in Cosmedin: Piazza Bocca della Verità, 18.
S. Maria in Domnica: Piazza della Navicella, 10.
S. Maria in Trastevere: Via della Paglia, 14c.
S. Maria in Vallicella: Piazza della Chiesa Nuova.
S. Maria sopra Minerva: Piazza della Minerva, 35.
S. Martino ai Monti: Viale Monte Oppio, 28.
SS. Nereo e Achilleo: Via delle Terme di Caracalla, 28.
S. Onofrio: Piazza S. Onofrio, 2.
Pantheon: Piazza della Rotonda.
S. Pietro in Montorio: Piazza S. Pietro in Montorio.
S. Pietro in Vincoli: Piazza S. Pietro in Vincoli, 4a.
S. Paolo alle Tre Fontane: Località Tre Fontane.
S. Prassede: Via di S. Prassede, 9a.
S. Prisca: Via S. Prisca, 11.
S. Pudenziana: Via Urbana, 161.
SS. Quattro Coronati: Via SS. Quattro, 20.
S. Saba: Piazza G. L. Bernini, 2.
S. Sabina: Piazza Pietro d'Illiria, 2.
S. Silvestro in Capite: Piazza S. Silvestro.
S. Sisto vecchio: Piazzale Numa Pompilio, 8.
S. Stefano Rotondo: Via S. Stefano Rotondo.
S. Susanna: Via XX Settembre, 14.
Trinità dei Monti: Piazza Trinità dei Monti.
S. Vitale: Via Nazionale, 194b.

CATACOMBS

Ciriaca: Piazzale S. Lorenzo, 3.
Dei Giordani: Via Taro.
Domitilla: Via delle Sette Chiese, 282.
Pretestato: Via Appia Pignatelli, 1.
Priscilla: Via Salaria, 430.
S. Agnese: Via Nometana, 349.
S. Callisto: Via Appia Antica, 110.
S. Felicita: Via Simeto, 2.
S. Pancrazio: Piazza S. Pancrazio, 5.
S. Sebastiano: Via Appia Antica, 132.

N. B.: *The catacombs of Santa Felicita, of Pretestato and of Giordani are not open to the public. Special permits are necessary for visits.*

THE "FOUR SIDED" CHRISTIAN IN THE ETERNAL CITY

BASILICA DI SAN PIETRO

SAN CRISOGONO

SANTO STEFANO ROTONDO

S. MARIA DELLA CONCEZIONE
detta I CAPPUCCINI

SANTA SUSANNA

SANTA FRANCESCA ROMANA,
detta anche SANTA MARIA NOVA

SAN PIETRO IN MONTORIO

SANTA MARIA DELL'ANIMA

SAN BARTOLOMEO
ALL'ISOLA

SANTA PRASSEDE

TRINITÀ DEI MONTI

SANT'IGNAZIO
DI LOYOLA

SANTA MARIA SOPRA MINERVA

PANTHEON

SAN VITALE

SAN CLEMENTE

CIRIACA

SAN CALLISTO

SAN LORENZO FUORI LE MURA

SAN SILVESTRO IN CAPITE

SANTA MARIA IN DOMNICA

SANTA MARIA ANTIQUA

SANTA MARIA
IN TRASTEVERE

SANT'ANDREA
DELLA VALLE

SANTA CECILIA

SAN GIOVANNI E PAOLO

SAN CARLO AL CORSO

SAN SISTO VECCHIO

SANTA PUDENZIANA

SAN PIETRO IN VINCOLI

SAN LUCA E MARTINA

SANTA FELICITA

SAN MARTINO AI MONTI

SANT'AGOSTINO

S. MARIA D'ARA COELI

SS. COSMA E DAMIANO

SAN GIOVANNI IN LATERANO

SANTA MARIA MAGGIORE

BASILICA DEI SANTI APOSTOLI   **PRETESTATO**

SANTI QUATTRO CORONATI

SANTI NEREO E ACHILLEO

SANT'ANDREA AL QUIRINALE

SAN MARCO

SANTA SABINA

AN PANCRAZIO

SANTA MARIA
DELLA PACE

SAN SABA

SANT'ONOFRIO

SAN LUIGI
DEI FRANCESI

SANT'AGNESE IN AGONE

AN GIORGIO IN VELABRO

SAN LORENZO IN DAMASO

SAN MARCELLINO
E PIETRO

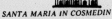

SANTA MARIA IN COSMEDIN

SANTA MARIA DEL POPOLO

SANTA PRISCA

SAN MARCELLO

SANTA CROCE
IN GERUSALEMME

DOMITILLA

SANTA COSTANZA

PRISCILLA

LA CHIESA DEL GESÙ

LA CHIESA NUOVA
o S. MARIA IN VALLICELLA

SANTA MARIA DEGLI ANGELI

SANT'ANASTASIA

SAN PAOLO ALLE TRE FONTANE

SAN GREGORIO MAGNO

DEI GIORDANI

SANTA AGNESE

SAN GIOVANNI A PORTA LATINA   SAN SEBASTIANO

BASILICA DI SAN PAOLO

INDEX